# Finding Fantastic Joy

In her book, Leah Johnson takes the same tools that enabled her "success addiction" as an elected official and uses them to build a redemptive campaign plan for herself and her family. I've always thought of campaigns as a way to heal communities. The author shows how those same strategies can be used by anyone to create joy and healing in their own lives, too.

**JEFF BRIDGES** Colorado State Senator

In *Finding Fantastic Joy*, Leah Johnson reveals her real power: telling the whole truth in a way that inspires. Johnson's memoir is a true heroine's journey, and it serves as a spark for others to do the sometimes scary work of beginning within. Johnson reminds us that seeking external validation is its own addiction, and she shows us how to break the cycle, claim our stories, and redefine winning.

**CYNDI GUESWEL** Founder, Only to Grow

Sometimes shattering the glass ceiling leaves you bruised and bloody. Leah's journey starts with a heartbreaking story of the collateral damage that comes with trying to compensate for internal strife by striving for (and earning) external accolades. The poignancy of *Finding Fantastic Joy*, though, is all about the path to redemption, forgiveness, and a redefined version of success. Leah expertly weaves together a framework anyone can use to start the important work of breaking cycles of trauma and cultivating a meaningful and joyful life. Ultimately, fantastic joy can't be defined by anyone else's standards but our own.

**ALLISON SEABECK** Mom Extraordinaire, CEO, and investor in accelerating businesses

*Finding Fantastic Joy* is equal parts love, pain, redemption, family, journey, discovery, humor, and rebirth. For those asking life's biggest questions, Leah's journey and plan for life can help you find direction.

**TOM LUCERO** Former University of Colorado Regent

As someone in recovery myself, I found this book so relatable. It is a quick read with huge impact and insight that will bring value for many, especially women navigating motherhood and career aspirations. Leah tells her story in a straightforward, energetic manner, weaving together her journey in both a spiritual and practical way. The "campaign" approach she takes is a fresh spin on steps to recovery, and as someone who also puts a huge (over) emphasis on achievement in my life, I found it to be a great tool in my approach to recovery. Leah's story is brave and will surely inspire others.

**JENNA DONEEN** Fantastic Mom, Creative Director of Life

Leah's journey and honesty profoundly impacted me as a driven professional who shared her addictions to success and winning at all costs. As she so eloquently describes, we could all benefit from a vision of ourselves by developing a self-advocacy campaign. The use of campaign techniques and her reawakening of spirituality to facilitate her journey to finding fantastic joy is something we can all emulate. If we did, I could imagine a more vibrant dialogue between the tribes that currently exist in today's political landscape that, as she states, "are not the narratives of reality!"

**BILLY HORTON** Democratic Strategist, Founder, Hard Count, Inc.

After 20 years of working in politics, Leah Johnson has crafted the most vital campaign message of her life in this story of finding herself and getting her joy back. My heart was moved as she shared difficult early life experiences and the resulting trauma and addictions. She eloquently lays out a roadmap to recovery that we can all learn from. This authentic and raw account of the author's journey to joy will be an encouragement to many.

**PAULA WOODWARD** Rockstar Mom, conservative thought leader, and small business owner

finding
fantastic
joy

LEAH JOHNSON

# finding fantastic joy

## HOW BUILDING A SELF-ADVOCACY CAMPAIGN LED ME OUT OF DARKNESS

modern wisdom
PRESS

**ᘉᘉ**
modern wisdom
P R E S S

Modern Wisdom Press
Boulder, Colorado, USA
www.modernwisdompress.com

Published 2022
Cover Design: Karen Sperry Design
Authors' photos courtesy of Jordan Jennings

**DISCLAIMER**
Neither the author nor the publisher assume any
responsibility for errors, omissions, or contrary
interpretations of the subject matter within.

**MEDICAL DISCLAIMER**
The information in this book is a result of years of practical
experience by the author. This information is not intended
as a substitute for the advice provided by your physician or
other healthcare professional. Do not use the information
in this book for diagnosing or treating a health problem or
disease, or prescribing medication or other treatment.

For my Mom.
Healing and forgiveness are choices, too.
I feel them both in your energy around me,
and I love you.

# contents

# foreword

---

*By Colorado State Representative Shannon Bird*

t he book you are holding is a beautiful story that will show you that, even though none of us has control over the events we will face in our lives, we always have control over how we respond to them. Importantly, you will walk through a poignant illustration that hard, painful periods in our lives are not a guarantee of a lifelong hurt but rather can be circumstances that mold you into a stronger, wiser, more loving version of your former self. These are lessons we need to know and to believe can be true even for ourselves.

I am a current Representative in the Colorado General Assembly and a former member of my city council. Prior to serving in elected office, I worked as a commercial and corporate finance attorney for a large law firm in the Denver area. Before going to law school, I earned a Master's degree in finance and an MBA. Like Leah, I have always worked hard and pushed to do more.

My family was heavily influenced by my grandmother, who has since passed away. She was part of a large Irish-Catholic family. She was raised in serious poverty with an alcoholic father during the Great Depression. Her upbringing loomed large in my family. My grandmother emerged from her youth toughened and with high expectations for her children and grandchildren. She was determined that none of us would ever have lives threatened by poverty or alcoholism. I adored my grandmother and was motivated and inspired by her. Others in my family, very close to me, were overwhelmed by her fierceness. Their hurt lingers on today.

Leah's story resonated with me.

Early in Leah's life, she had a painful relationship with her mother. Leah's response was to work harder to prove her worthiness to be loved. Indeed, her efforts were rewarded with enviable academic and professional success. Unfortunately, however, they did not fix her relationship with her mother. Undaunted, Leah continued in her efforts. Over the years, instead of yielding the intended result of a mended fundamental relationship, her ambition pushed her to the brink. Leah, however, did not allow these circumstances to define her. Leveraging her spirituality, tenacity, community, and inner wisdom, Leah rewrote her story and followed another path to joy.

I first met the talented author of this book when I enrolled in a program called Emerge. Emerge focused on training women in the Democratic party to run for political office. By the time I enrolled, Leah was an alum and had run a successful campaign to join her local city council. She was held up as a shining example of someone who stood up for her values and who could even thrive politically in a more conservative environment.

No one in our circles knew the struggles Leah was working through at the time. What we saw was an independent and well-respected woman who knew how to get things done. She was always quick to offer advice and to show others how to be successful.

We all have family backgrounds that impact who we are today and that continue to influence our daily lives. Though my family story is different from Leah's, her journey and desire to recalibrate her ambitions caused a healthy self-reflection in me. As I read on, I found myself saying, "me too." We need others to be vulnerable and brave and to share their stories. I believe this can be a catalyst for us to look at our own circumstances and choices in a new, helpful light.

Leah's book provides a concrete example of how to emerge from early trauma. For those of us who believe that our self-worth is dependent upon how high we climb on the ladder, she shows us another way. Each of us has inherent value that does not depend upon the letters behind our name or the professional heights we reach.

I have always believed that early trauma and struggle do not necessarily define people as victims for the rest of their lives.

These challenges, if met with the insight and gratitude illustrated by the author, can be part of what brings you to the successes you will enjoy in the future and to the happiness you can enjoy today. Leah's path is remarkable, and her work to grow is a guiding light for the rest of us.

Shannon Bird
Colorado State Representative

# introduction

———

there is an inherent juxtaposition in writing this book. At its core, it's about my own personal journey as a person who struggled so much with the need to succeed, so much with my fear of failure, that it absolutely consumed my life and almost killed me. It swallowed my soul and my relationships, it made me sad, it made me drink, and it was all rooted in a trauma response that never had been addressed or acknowledged in a healthy fashion. Yet the mere action of writing a book comes with a connotation of success or failure.

For me, though, if my dad and eighth grade English teacher are the only ones who purchase this book, it will still be a success because I did it. For the first time, I have taken on a task in life that was about nothing but who I am at my core. The success is that I did it, and I did it for me. With that being said, I hope dearly that others take the parts of my story that resonate with them and use them to empower their own lives in a meaningful way.

When given the choice for over a decade to find different paths toward happiness, I dug in deeper with the need to prove something, the need to be the most successful ever. (And I honestly can't even tell you what that means. I just know it was a thought that went through my head regularly.) Further weighing on my addiction to success was my instinctive reaction every time people expressed concern over my general state of being or my overall health because I would double down, looking for an even bigger success. That was always the answer, I thought; that is what would make me happy. This need to accomplish the perfect image in my head, even though I was a relatively accomplished individual, was all-consuming and never realistic. As you can imagine, when I fell short of the unattainable, which I often did, other coping mechanisms set in. And it became a vicious cycle that spiraled one way: down. It was brutal and dark. Death was a real possibility, and looking back, I am not totally sure how I made it out alive. But I did. Ultimately, what I did is choose my life, my children, and my little family unit that I love so dearly and gives me immeasurable joy.

About a year and a half after I stopped it all and reevaluated, I went on a trip to New Orleans with three girlfriends. We had rich experiences in the city and surrounding areas. The food, the people, the art, the culture, the architecture, the history, and the swamp: All were all wonderful. When I am traveling, I am in my sweet spot. (Lots more about this later.) Traveling truly makes me dig deep and appreciate who I am and what I have, all while growing and exposing my senses to new places, new tastes, and new smells. It feeds my soul in a way nothing else can; I need to roam outside the familiar to grow and change.

Our last night there, we walked the streets on the edges of the French Quarter, those places filled with character, where the spirit of the city oozes out of the buildings, the streets, and the people. As we strolled, a bookstore that we had passed many times without noticing came into my view in a new way. As we walked toward it, I could see it had a feel of hipster meets Creole meets voodoo meets magic. A man was sitting outside with an old typewriter, one from my grandparents' generation. His gentleness was palpable from six feet away (this was Covid times after all). Just being in the same orbit as he was made me feel safe. The universe was saying: pay attention to this moment because it matters.

He said to us, "Would you like me to write you a poem?"

"Sure, how does it work?" I asked him.

His dark brown eyes melted over me. "You give me a word, and then I write a poem, and if you like it, you pay me what you think it is worth."

Recognizing an opportunity to say "yes" to something in life, I wholeheartedly agreed. I gave him the word "JOY." We then proceeded into the bookstore. I knew I had $20 cash in my wallet, so I settled on that to give him. As it turned out, it would be hard to put a value on something so priceless.

After 10 minutes, I exited the bookstore. The poet asked if I would sit down so he could read it to me. "Of course!" I threaded one leg and then the next into the bright yellow picnic table where he was seated. He pulled his mask down, revealing a charming grin, and read:

> fantastic
> feelings
> of invincibility
> riding that
> cosmic wave
> they say it goes by fast
> but when you find
> that mental sweet spot
> you find yourself
> touching infinity
>
> — eq carter
> frenchman st
> nola
> oct 16 2020

I was frozen and overcome with emotion all at once. How had this tender-hearted man on the corner of Frenchman Street and Chartres Street so profoundly nailed the emotions I was feeling?

My friend asked the poet and me, "What was the word? Fantastic?"

"No," the poet said with a sheepish grin. "The word she gave me was joy."

My friend laughed a little. "That is crazy. I thought for sure it was fantastic because you say it all the time, Leah."

Fantastic. Joy. It seemed I may have found it.

At that moment, it was clearer to me than at any other point in my life that I was in the exact right place and on the exact right path. My story had really just begun. I had learned what mattered to me most and how to build a campaign for myself that led me to a life filled with fantastic joy.

This journey, and the things I have learned, are not unique although many of the subjects in this book are not spoken about near enough in our society. This is a human story of learning self-advocacy. It is a memoir of discovering that when you pick yourself first, you allow yourself greater opportunities to flourish, and all those around you benefit. It is my story, and at its lows, I cringe with embarrassment and regret, but at its highs, my sense of my own humanity is restored. On this journey, I seek a path that ensures my children don't have to know the generational threads of trauma and addiction. Healing and forgiveness are choices, and for the good of my world and my children's world, I finally chose the opportunity to do life differently: to make myself happier, and ultimately to find fantastic joy.

# darkness

**m**ost days, I just want to kill myself, and a few times I tried.

The need to succeed is all-consuming, deep inside of me; I cannot control it. I am sad, the kind of sad that is in your bones. The kind of sad people can see deep in my eyes, the kind of sadness that day by day chips away grains of my soul until I feel like nothing more than a shell. In my need to keep filling my vessel with anything that will take away the pain, I seek the next success. Sometimes that works, but it is never enough.

So, naturally, I try another way to make the emptiness stop: alcohol. All I want is a reprieve for just a moment so I can be still and not hate myself. But it never works. Often a new success is fleeting, and substances add to the guilt and pain I already feel when it doesn't endure. But all the same, I seek the next achievement, the next win, at any cost. And the pieces left of me after that are few and far between.

As a professional woman in the American political system, my goal is always the next glass ceiling. I need the next thing to prove, like heroin addicts need their next hit. Through children, bad decisions, days where I can't get out of bed, I hold onto this need to do the next big thing. That's what will make it better, I am certain. That is what will make me happy.

Gratefully, mental health has become more of a public conversation, and I know that it is something I need to address personally. So, I try. I have tried for a decade. Those years of back and forth with doctors and therapists' diagnosis after diagnosis: "It's depression; no, it's anxiety; no, it's this; no, it's that." A drug here and another drug there, but nothing makes the pain go away. I have babies and face postpartum depression so debilitating that I spend more time in bed than not. But I muster every ounce of strength to put my best foot forward when my absence would be noticed because I must prove myself.

The babies are beautiful, and I love them so deeply; it's visceral. But the pain surrounds me and them. Guilt punches me in the stomach every day, telling me what a terrible mom I am, how I am just repeating cycles of pain. I double over with guilt about what they are eating or not eating, guilt about their education and growth, guilt about saying "yes," or saying "no." Guilt about them seeing me not together and not successful enough. Just guilt.

And that guilt carries over into my work and involvement in my community. I feel guilty for not being perfect and able to do it all. I can get elected to public office, get the promotion, get the prestigious award, and none of it sticks. That guilt sits just below the surface in everything I do. But the belief that the right success, the right accolade will cure it all, accompanies the guilt. And the guilt is kindling for the addiction to achievement.

One day I will be governor, one day I will be in the State House, one day I will make it back to Washington, D.C., one day I will be President of the Moon. There is really no success that will ever fill the hole inside. So, I drink.

Occasionally in all this, I come up for air and do something that fills me up in a good way. I find a moment to connect more deeply with the universe, engage in a family trip that brings joy, dive into an exercise and nutrition plan that promises to make me feel better. And though those moments are deep and meaningful and though they matter, they are like putting a pebble over a geyser. The sadness just keeps gushing.

I hold onto these moments, though. I collect them in a jar in my mind, with the belief that if I can gather enough happy pebbles to cash in, I might fully be happy. But my sadness may as well be an abusive lover, its grip is so strong. And I just keep coming back to it over and over again. My sadness tells me, as my mother did, that I am not enough and the only way I will be enough is if I am the most successful ever.

Of course, the truth is no one can do it all, but I will not hear such things. So, my marriage suffers, I lack deep meaningful friendships, my family relationships suffer, and it becomes clear that I am on an island, not too far off shore, but distant enough to know what a long swim it will take to return to the mainland.

I have a choice. Do I stay out there in isolation, wallowing in my sorrow and self-hatred until I wither to nothing? Or do I leave that all on the island, jump into the water, and swim? I'm going to have to swim faster and harder than I have for anything because, at this point, my life depends on it.

I'm the only person who can cross these waters. I have to believe in myself, and the only way to do that is to abandon all that other garbage on the island and go. (Maybe I'll light a match for good measure as I leave.)

The only person who is going to advocate for me in the deepest way is me. No one can make my leap into the water or swim with all my might for something different. Joy is actually mine for the taking, but the onus is on me to embark on what would turn out to be a profound spiritual journey and to know there is contentment and happiness on the other side. At the core of getting there is learning how to be an advocate for my own joy, with a commitment unlike I have devoted to anything else in my life.

# addiction

One of the things that drives me insane about the world is how people go straight to focusing on an addiction and think that is the problem. I'm not saying addictions can't cause problems themselves as they have in my life, but addictions are symptoms. They point us to deep-seated suffering inside us. It took strength and self-awareness for me even to begin to understand how all the pieces were connected. Struggles on the surface appeared to be the problems, but a deeper dive was required to see the real challenge. In my experience, stopping an addiction isn't easily accomplished by having others, or even myself, talk at the addiction. The phrase "You have a drinking problem" is nails on a chalkboard to me. These days, every time I hear that, I promptly respond with "I am sure she is dealing with some pretty deep traumatic and emotional wounds, so before we start labeling the 'problem,' let's offer some grace to her as she travels." I believe, had I felt a little more compassion and a little less judging on my own journey, I might have taken some different turns.

For years, people, especially my family, talked at my problem, never acknowledging that my struggle was rooted far deeper than a few too many drinks. Naming the symptom as a problem just seemed to make everyone else in the situation feel better about it. Meanwhile, I was filled with shame, guilt, and judgment, and fear of the one thing I dreaded more than anything: failure. The only thing I knew to do that countered a fear so deep that it would bring me to my breaking point was push myself to that breaking point to succeed.

I know now that I have a trauma problem that created a most unhealthy, unrealistic addiction to achievement, to winning. This is one of those cases where semantics matter. For years, people looked at my addictions as the problem. These compulsions were no doubt mental, emotional, and physical blocks keeping me from changing for the better, but they came from somewhere deep inside me. And more than anything, I wrestled with the fear of failure that sent me so deeply into the abyss that I almost did not come out alive.

My trauma problem started early with my mom. The truth is, though others may have seen our relationship differently, my mom didn't like me very much. I know this because she told me so. She said it when she was dying. As I tended to her on her deathbed, stricken with cancer, she told me point blank that I was a disappointment. I looked at her, and all I could muster was, "I'm sorry, Mom." She was short on words at that point, but long on emotion. I reached toward her with a washcloth in my hand, only for her to turn away.

This wasn't the first time she told me I was a disappointment.

She said it when I was a third grader. On a seemingly normal school morning, she came into my room berating me yet again for having not picked up. As she threw things and screamed at me for being an ungrateful, horrible child, I was overcome by the feeling that would return time and again as I grew up, the sense that an internal fortress was being built, brick by brick, to protect myself from her wrath.

That fortress was only so strong, though. On this particular occasion, she told me the adoption agency would be there to get me when I got home as that is where children like me go. You can imagine my dismay when it ended up being a snow day, and we were sent home early. As I left that building, I felt as if I was walking the plank right into the alligator's mouth.

Over the years, out of self-protection, I engaged less and less with my mom. This left only one parent to go to, which created a host of other problems. As I grew closer to my dad, seeking some sort of refuge in the battlefield that was my home, our connection only made things worse for both of us.

One fall day, my parents sat me down in the living room. Feeling stiff, on the already stiff furniture in our home, they told me they would be separating.

I was flooded with relief. I quickly imagined a life free of my mother's tirades against me. It didn't last long. After my father left the room, my mom wasted no time in telling me who was to blame for the separation: me. It was my fault, and she wanted to ensure that point was not missed. My parents never actually separated, which is another story, but my supposed role in their dysfunction from that point on was made clear.

She made sure I knew she didn't like me when I was in college. I called her to tell her I got an "A." I found a bench amongst Boston cobblestones and brownstones on Bay Street Road in the shade of the trees and the buildings and in the crisp fall air. It was an idyllic setting, a perfect place to sit and share the good news with my mom. How could this time not be different? How could she not tell me she was proud of me? That she loved me? Well, this time, she went big. She launched into a monologue, ranting about the entire family. And then there was the kicker: "I wish I had never had you as a daughter."

The words stung as I sat there trying to process them. I imagine she had said them before, but I remember this time vividly. The place, the air, the smells, the day that had seemed so perfect minutes before now came crashing down. She had said what I always felt she had wanted to say, and those words rang in my body over and over again.

Really, who says that?

My mother said it after I was raped. When I was home one summer during college, my parents noticed that I had become withdrawn, and I was participating heavily in activities like partying unlike I ever had before. When pressed, I shared that I had been sexually assaulted while away at school. My mom looked at me and simply said, "That is your fault if you were drinking." She then sat there sobbing, not because of what had happened to her daughter, but because of what her daughter had done.

The whole thing made no sense at the time and made even less sense in the months to follow when she even refused to speak with me. This just confirmed her dislike and disgust of me. Somehow, I was to blame for having sex forced upon me.

She said it when I had a miscarriage. My husband Mike and I started trying to have children about a year before she passed. We all knew her death was looming, and the thought of grand-children excited her. When I became pregnant, I thought this would be the thing that would finally make her like me. That pregnancy would be unsuccessful. I sought comfort from her, as I mistakenly did every single time. Surely, as a mother, she would understand the pain I was feeling. But she was not capable of providing that comfort. Instead, she said, "Because of your miscarriage, I won't ever meet grandchildren. Leah, you have failed me."

If you asked me when I was 10, 14, 18, 22, or 28, or on her deathbed when I was 30, does your mother like you, I would have said, "No, in fact I think she hates me." I honestly cannot recall a day when I woke up believing my mom liked me.

She found all sorts of ways to say it: I was a disappointment, I wasn't meeting her expectations, she didn't like the way I was doing something, I let her down, I was ungrateful. The fascinating, if not all that surprising, thing is that despite all this rejection, her approval was all I sought. Even after her death, I would dig deep, reaching a breaking point just to do things so my mom would like me. Or so anyone would like me. So, maybe I could like myself.

When I was a kid, and especially as a teenager, I felt the pressure to be so many things. A leader constantly pushing up to the next level, such as student body president and the senior class president, always visible, always driven. I was the all-star golfer, determined to receive a golf scholarship, and the academic leader always expected to get the best grades. I volunteered and was on the debate team. I was dead set on being the all-star kid. I had to be the child who had it all together, accomplished everything, and won all the awards. I had to be, what was in my mind, perfect. This way, maybe just once, one of those accomplishments would make my mom like me.

These beliefs did not go away as I grew older and the world just got bigger. Opportunities abounded, and I always sought the next opportunity to define my résumé, to be impressive, and to prove that I was truly something. As events unfolded in my life, external success became nothing more than a shield to protect me from the truth of what I was dealing with at my core. Accomplishment became the drug of choice that allowed me to get through the trauma problem I had.

After my mom died, I decided to run for the City Council in my hometown of Loveland, Colorado. I told myself my mother had prepared me for campaigning as there was nothing anyone could say about me that would sting more or hurt more than what she had said. After hearing my mom say she wished I wasn't her daughter, it was hard to be bothered by any accusations they would lob at me. The ironic thing was that at the same time, my run for City Council was maybe my greatest attempt to prove that I was worthy and convince her to like me. I won the race and served for four years, which was not only all-consuming but a very public success.

Of course, she wasn't there to find failures in this achievement because she was dead. But it was after her death that my ache for her acceptance overtook me. Now, I would never get the chance to show her that one thing, whatever it was, that would finally make her give me a hug and say, "I love you." So, the addiction persisted. Smack dab in the middle of the "greatest success of my life," I sought even bigger opportunities, including seriously considering running for a higher office, all while being incapacitated by depression. Winning another campaign, I thought, would bring me the external love that I so desperately sought.

Add to that, everything I was then being told about my career. Push harder; women can do it all. In my run for City Council, I had a miscarriage the day ballots dropped. A day later, I left the emergency room with horse-pill sized Tylenol, and I went straight to a Get Out the Vote rally where I was surrounded by dozens of people, and not one person knew what I'd just experienced. I pressed on, dead set to show that I could break my own little glass ceiling. And though I went on to get elected, I felt more alone than I had at any other moment in my life. I had yet another success, and it surely would make me feel better. So, I buried my second miscarriage deep inside. I had things to do and no time for grief.

I kept pushing and ended up having a baby while serving on the City Council. Glass ceiling shattered again! First woman to have a baby while being elected to public office in my community. Great idea? Not so much.

By this time, I think it was all just starting to catch up with me. The postpartum depression that ensued was debilitating, and even while I tried to get help, it just worsened. My existence went to nothing but darkness. I was so low, and I knew nowhere to go. Even my addiction to achievement had been swallowed by it. I was done. Of course, it always has to get far worse before it gets better.

So, I went deeper into the darkness. If I admitted something was wrong, if I admitted I had underlying problems, if I admitted I needed help, then I would be a failure. I would wake up nearly every morning with a string of thoughts running through my head: "I wish I were dead." "I have to keep pushing to success, so I am not a failure." "If I quit or pause even for a minute, I will be even more of a failure." And on, and on. I truly believed I could just push through and find the next success that would jolt me out of the darkness. Occasionally, a fleeting thought in the back of my brain would say, "You need to stop. You need help." I should have stopped and told myself I needed help many years before I did, but my fear of failure had permeated my entire being. I honestly don't think stopping was possible.

Then, one night I took a half a bottle of Tylenol on top of copious amounts of alcohol. I woke up in convulsions. My liver seemed to be shutting down. My husband woke up and sat with me. Having watched the spiral for a few years, I honestly don't think he was even surprised. He insisted on calling an ambulance, but as I was coherent enough, I convinced him not to, knowing it would be hard to hide a 72-hour psychiatric hold in the hospital from the external world. So, we sat in silence, Mike keeping a watchful eye if anything changed. His look and touch were that of stern compassion. The next morning, he simply said, "Leah, things need to change. You need to get help." That's the first time I remember hearing him say those words, although I have no doubt he told me many times before.

Even though I was scared to death at the thought that I might have actually killed myself, that wouldn't have been enough to shake the deep-seated belief that if I asked for help and admitted to something other than strength and success, I would be a failure. And I announced my re-election bid for Loveland City Council shortly thereafter. I simply could not admit I was drowning.

As it turns out, one more goal put out there, one more accomplishment to collect, didn't solve anything, and the next few months after my first suicide attempt, there was another and, through it all, a constant deep, dark sadness. It would take a statement that only one person could deliver to finally make me admit I needed help. One evening, Mike said, "Leah, you cannot live like this anymore. You have to get help. I can't do this anymore, and I will not let our kids live like this." That was the dagger to my heart: Our children.

I deserved better than what I was giving myself, and my children deserved a mother who was present and at minimum not desperately sad. Suddenly, the definition of success began to shift. It became what I was going to do for myself to be my best self for my children. Success was, in fact, turning into my previous definition of failure: admitting I couldn't do it all, and I needed help. So, I said to Mike, "Call my dad. I want him to take me to rehab tonight."

And then things changed. Most people who go to rehab say the hardest thing to give up is a substance. But alcohol was easy for me because, at the core, my addiction was to success, to winning. The most important and difficult thing I did in rehab, and quite possibly in my life, was to write a press release, withdrawing from my re-election at my post as a local City Councilor. And you know what, the whole thing seemed to transpire as a non-event. All this built up in my head, and when I said I was withdrawing so I could prioritize my family, people generally supported it. Though some had a glimpse into the struggles I faced, few knew how dark my world was. So, outwardly, it seemed like a good decision all around.

Sending that press release was the single scariest thing I had ever done. However, the process alerted me to the fact that I had to thoroughly redefine what success looked like for me, and the only way to do that was to start over. I would need to build a healthy relationship to achievement and one that honored who I am as a human. I began then for the first time in my life to build success from the inside out. I had spent a career advocating for causes and people outside of myself. What I needed to do was build a campaign for me. I needed to learn what self-advocacy looked like, and then and only then could I advocate for others again.

# the plan

I have worked in campaign politics my entire career. My career started in high school, and I was hooked. Working on a local State Senate campaign, I was brought into the fold early. And the thing about campaigns is there are never enough people to do all the work that needs to be done, so if you want a lot of responsibility and are capable of following through, you get the job, especially on the local races. And that's how it began for me: meeting with the local newspaper about ad opportunities, organizing parades, and just being present and around the strategy all the time. That was nearly 25 years ago, and I have been involved in some campaign, in some capacity, nearly every election cycle since.

Over the years, there is no doubt that my love of politics (maybe even an addiction in itself) fueled my need to succeed. To be clear, though, at the time, I didn't call it success in my head although it represented that in a meaningful way. It was a drive to change the world for the better, and I believed that with every ounce of my being. In college, I got a taste of the big leagues. Interning for the John Kerry for President campaign in New Hampshire, that was as big as it got. The money, the notoriety, the national press, and the national consultants that come with these campaigns. The Granite State in a Presidential primary is retail politics at its finest and a far different space than the underfunded, understaffed, local campaigns of my high school days. I remember the creepy Fox News reporters (even then), and my starstruck moments. One day, they piled us interns onto Kerry's tour bus. The candidate and the staff in the front, the press in the back with us sandwiched firmly in the middle. It was a dream come true for a kid from Loveland. I was part of democracy in the making.

I went on after college to work campaigns in Georgia and South Dakota, returning to these smaller races with positions and feelings of responsibility. In both cases, I was hired as a Field Director of sorts, and quickly found myself doing a million other jobs. Fundraising, management, organizing, events, and press. Serving as the on the record spokesperson in West River, South Dakota, wasn't exactly what I signed up for, but more responsibility meant more success. I was exposed to people who could help me keep climbing the ladder, and I was building my resume.

To my surprise, that small South Dakota campaign ended up being a ticket to access to the most historical campaign we have seen in American history. As I was transitioning from one campaign to another, my boss from South Dakota called and asked what I was doing that weekend: February 9, 2007. I did have plans because that was my birthday weekend. He explained to me that I needed to drive to Iowa at once because there was this first-term Senator from Illinois who was announcing his candidacy for President of the United States, and they needed volunteers. I was in my car and on my way within the day.

I hit the road with the hope that I could land the next gig on my path to changing the world. As I sped east on I-80, I had chills throughout my being knowing that I was going to be part of Barack Obama's announcing he was running for president. I had done advance for big events like this before, and I had become pretty familiar with Presidential campaigns. This one felt different. I walked into the basketball arena in Ames, Iowa. It was empty, yet it had the feeling of opportunity. At the top of the first tier of the arena, another intern about my age and I were introduced to the Secret Service agents.

They simply said we were needed to escort the Obamas down the stairs. Yeah. Okay, I can do that. Inside my head, I was screaming, "What the hell, how did this just happen, just pinch me now. What the—Holy, no way—AAAHHH!" And I did. I walked down the aisle standing a foot from the soon-to-be greatest president (in my humble opinion) of my life as he prepared to take the stage and announce he was running for President of the United States of America. All the pain that came from my drive to find success couldn't take away how damn cool that experience was. Being part of this momentous event ultimately landed me a job in D.C., which furthered my developing the skills to give voice to the issues I care about. I would later come to see that these tools could be used to build a self-advocacy campaign for me.

My last stints in national politics involved more of the same: a lot of responsibility, a lot of learning, great for my résumé, building that momentum for success and accomplishment. During these early years in my career, there were certainly great moments and many of them. They taught me a lot, afforded me terrific mentors, and connected me with people I respect greatly in the business. And even though the challenge of trauma sat just below the surface, I was also far away from my hometown, my family, and my mom. Failure was more forgiving out there where anonymity was possible. It was really when I landed back in Loveland that the overwhelming need to succeed took over, and I felt I had something to prove, especially to my mom.

As soon as I returned home, I started advocating for all the things I thought would make my community better. Downtown revitalization, the needs of the homeless, and affordable housing. I ran for City Council on these issues, a campaign I knew how to run. Extra earned media for the things I cared about started showing up, people began to organize in ways they hadn't for things I cared about, and at one point, I even had a regular column in a local paper. When it came to running a campaign to get Leah Johnson elected to City Council, it turns out I was pretty good at that. I won with 63 percent of the vote.

What I realize now is that I did it all backward. The first campaign I should have ever run was the campaign for me. I needed a campaign creating strength from within, to become strong inside before I let the external world tell me who I was. But, for so long, I could not see that. All I could see was that the next success meant I wasn't a failure. The next success shielded me, showing the outside world that I was fine while I was actually falling apart. But success is an artificial support, and failure a very real fear. And that trauma problem wasn't going away by hiding behind things that really didn't heal my soul.

Hitting send on the press release to withdraw from my race for re-election changed it all. Whenever I sent a press release, I would hover over the send button a little longer than normal. Because hitting send on a press release has power. It has the ability to create a story and change the narrative. It is a tool that I do not take for granted. So, as I hesitated before finally hitting send, I knew I was fundamentally changing the course of who I was. It allowed me to hit the reset button in my life and do what I should have done a long time before: Build a campaign for me first to find the fantastic joy that I had been longing for my whole life.

So, then what?

Well, looking back, I took all the tools I'd developed from my two-decade career in politics and applied them to myself.

First, I needed to become the campaign manager of my own life. I needed to stop letting all the external factors determine what I did. The fear, the addictions, the judgment, the trauma, the fear of failure, the mom guilt: all of it had to go. I always said no one could run a better negative campaign against me than the one in my head, and I had done that for long enough. It was time for me to use the skills I had at my disposal to run a campaign for myself.

The best campaigns start with research. Though opposition research is important, the most vital thing is to do the research on the issue or person at hand. Knowing weaknesses and vulnerabilities and being prepared to talk about them and being proactive about how and when to talk about them is critical. In this case, the issue was me, and I needed to research myself; I needed to evaluate the good, the bad, and the ugly. It was time to look deep inside, truly understand where and what the trauma was and how to deal with it and learn to heal from it. I needed to not hate my mom. And I needed to stop feeling violated from the sexual assault and kept from truly getting close to anyone because of it. I needed to stop hating myself. I had to do the hard work of self-research and then create a plan for dealing with it all.

Once you know what you have to address, the next step is the messaging. I had to take back the message running in my head that I was a failure, that I was worthless, that I was a miserable excuse for a human and a terrible mom. Messaging is a powerful thing, especially the messaging we tell ourselves, and now as the campaign manager of my own life, I could no longer let the negative narrative control the story.

Once I had control of the narrative, I became laser-focused on what matters. All campaigns have to start with a focus. Most of the time it is a candidate, though often it's an issue. And for the sake of the analogy, the focal point was my kids. As the campaign manager of my own life, focusing on my kids as the center made sense. They meant everything to me and putting them at the heart of the campaign and building everything around them just made sense. It was like starting with your "Why." They are the why. I had to define what being a good mom was to me and determine how to build the healthiest, happiest relationships possible with them. Those commitments mattered most. In campaigning, it is critical to put your core priority first and build everything else around it.

After you have all that in place, you have to fund a campaign. What are the things that fill your bank and make you whole? My bank was filled by my connection to my spiritual beliefs and travel, two elements that are deeply connected for me. These intertwined resources needed to become priorities. "Funding" myself with what makes me feel whole allowed me to better and more intentionally spend resources on others. Focus on the things that fill you up, in a healthy, happy way, and do those more, so much more.

The last element of any good campaign is your grassroots work. Who are your allies? Build your advocacy networks and then know how to activate them. Or, in short, know who the people are that are in your corner and elevate them. Empower them to be part of your happiness journey.

Put this all together and you end up with one pretty solid campaign plan for yourself. It acknowledges who you are, fills you up, and allows you to operate in life from a position of strength because you are advocating for yourself first and then others second. And I can speak with great authority with the argument that if you don't take care of yourself first, there is really nothing left to give when it comes to the rest. And the point of personal self-destruction and demise is an awful place to be.

# research

So, we start with research and not opposition research although that is often the result of the "fun" unending ads leading up to any election. You need background research to make the best decisions as a campaign manager. There needs to be a deep understanding of the weaknesses that are associated with the campaign, so you can do one of two things: be proactive about getting the information out there or have a response ready when it comes. The proactive approach is usually preferable. That way you control the message. I will get back to that message thing in the next chapter, but first and foremost the research.

When I stepped back and reevaluated my life, I realized one very important thing: All sorts of things had happened to me, whether by my own hand or by others, or carried down through my DNA from those who had come before me. I had never fully acknowledged the scope of trauma and its impact on me. I needed to take a deep dive and know what these experiences were, so I could change the narrative. But if I didn't face that those pockets of acute pain existed, addressing them would be impossible.

In my mind, my overwhelming yearning for success was a trauma response that became an addiction. I heard a radio interview recently with an addiction specialist who talked about behavioral addictions as being the same as chemical ones. My behavioral addiction was success, the need to be seen, the constant striving to do the next thing in the most unhealthy and destructive way. I cannot stress enough that I did not know how to stop the need for accolades and achievement. Because I needed that dopamine high that came with that addiction, I needed a filler in the middle, the quick dopamine that came from the alcohol and the prescription drugs. These were my secondary addictions.

I had tried for a decade at least to fix everything clinically. When I went to the treatment facility, for the first time, I received a full assessment of why I was so deeply sad and what I could do to relieve the sadness. A genetic test could tell me which of the medications worked for me. SSRIs didn't (wouldn't that have been nice to know a decade before). I managed to advocate for myself to get the best care possible and had the Chief Clinical Officer assess the whole landscape of my mental health. After a few meetings, she said, matter of factly, "I believe your challenges are just chronic PTSD." My problems were a trauma response to the relationship with my mother and being sexually assaulted in college. And perhaps some generational trauma compiled on top of that. "Just" chronic PTSD. I honestly can't say I have ever been so relieved.

Now I had a basis for my behavior, and I felt armed with good information and research about where I was. I could honor my personal accountability and take the appropriate steps to stop the trauma response that was crushing my soul and slowly destroying my life. Also, my deepening spiritual beliefs told me this trauma spanned generations.

My real spiritual awakening started on a front porch of a 100-year-old home in downtown Loveland, Colorado. Up until this point, I would have said I didn't know what I believed and often probably said I didn't believe in anything. A friend of mine, seeing the emptiness in my being, suggested some books, Eckhart Tolle's *The Power of Now* and Don Miguel Ruiz's *The Four Agreements*. She also said there was a place she had gone in Mexico called Teotihuacan, and it was where the teachings of the Toltec came from and what was written about in the Four Agreements. She said the place had helped her connect with something greater. I bought the books immediately, and I booked a plane ticket to Mexico City three weeks later. I was ready.

This was right before children, in a time where we had decided we would start trying and my mother was clearly dying. I needed to do something differently, and a trip to Mexico, to possibly join a cult as my mother said, seemed like the prescription I needed. In my mom's defense, it was a little crazy, and from the outside, it may have seemed extreme. Healing doesn't happen without taking personal risks and getting out of your comfort zone, and this seemed just crazy enough that it might work. Though it wasn't an overnight spiritual awakening or a cult, it laid a new foundation, and a desire to return four more times, that would allow big personal growth and change over the next six years of my life. That moment on the porch would eventually give me the strength to say, "Enough," and change how I existed.

From my first trip to Teotihuacan, to my day-to-day spiritual practices (or lack thereof sometimes), my spiritual journey has really been key to me settling into myself, settling into my pain, settling into the anxiety and depression in a way that has allowed me to live and thrive. And not despite the trauma but with it in a healthy way. My deep spiritual belief is really about giving up control or admitting that I can't control everything, but if I trust and act with intention and gratitude, the universe will give back, in my experience, tenfold.

This understanding of letting go allowed me to understand how connected we are. By cleansing my soul on ancient sites in Mexico, I became aware of an energy there of the people who came before me, my ancestors. In my opinion, it is no coincidence that the general feelings and demeanors of family are passed down through the generations. It's not just your hair color and your skin color you get from ancestors; you also get the energy and the trauma and the experiences that shaped them. I could begin to feel the pains of generations of women who came before me. It became clearer than ever that the work I was doing to spiritually free my energy was help-ing those of the past and those of the future. And this deep spiritual and energetic connection created a space for the new Leah to exist with all the trauma and PTSD and not let it own me and control me but rather simply be part of a complex and beautiful human story.

Spirituality, a belief in something bigger, drives most of my decisions these days. I don't really believe in coincidences anymore and have a strong sense that all things are con-nected. With this in mind, I went to see a medium on that recent trip to New Orleans. I had never been to a medium before and honestly wasn't sure about the experience, but if I have learned anything, it's that saying yes to unique experi-ences seems to pay off. So, in I went. The first thing she did was ask me to name three people. My grandma was one.

I knew the rigidity of my grandmother, Dorothy, and the role addiction played in her life. She was of German descent and had a hardness about her that only comes from years of inter-nal struggles. When I think about my own journey, I often reflect on hers as well. The suffering that woman must have faced to get to where she was brought tears to my eyes. She didn't live in a time when people talked about their emotional pain. Writing a book like this wasn't an option. She lived in an era in which everything was swept under the rug. I feel fortu-nate to live in a time where I can deal with my feelings even if, at times, doing that seems overwhelmingly difficult.

When Grandma Dorothy came through, the room changed. It felt almost sunnier, and the halo around the medium's head became clear. My guard came down and the medium asked, "Do you have any questions for Dorothy?"

"You seemed to live such a hard, sometimes sad life. Are you happy?" I asked.

The medium said, "Dorothy says simply this is not for you to worry about. She lived in a different time, in a time where people had to be stoic. You get to live differently. You, young lady, get to find joy and heal. Go be happy."

The medium wagged her finger at me in a way that my grandmother used to. I could not walk out of that room without believing that I had just received a strong sign from the universe. I also couldn't leave without recognizing that what had occurred there had a lot to do with healing trauma. I point out the "universe moments" a lot these days, but these moments, these pivotal spaces where I question myself less and believe in myself more, are critical crumbs to pick up on the trail as I travel.

I have no doubt my mother experienced trauma, too. She never said so, exactly, but she gave enough hints over the years to indicate this. Looking back, it seems many of her actions were based in a trauma response. Research into yourself, and your past allows a new awareness of the suffering of those who came before you. For many years, all I was doing was operating in survival mode, the fight-or-flight mentality, and I realized that was likely where my mother was coming from, too. After I visited the medium, I looked at my mother with more compassion. I ached for the pain she felt and whatever was eating at her insides, making her so sad and mean.

Looking back at myself, I could easily see where and when it got worse: the triggers from the trauma and the need to cover it up with being outwardly perfect. The thing about trauma is it becomes a state of being, a place where you live and have no idea how to escape. So, you survive in a self-destructive cycle that brings more trauma and never allows you to heal. I just pushed, and pushed, and pushed until I had pushed myself to the breaking point. My life was in the balance if I didn't change, and the only way to get out ahead of that reality was to admit I couldn't do it all. I had to accept that I needed help. I needed to stop and withdraw from my re-election because stopping the trauma response of the drive for success was the only way I would survive. It was certainly the only way that I could regain my own internal message.

# messaging

So, what does a healthy relationship to success look like for me? It's not like drinking. I can't just quit success. As I said, once I realized I needed to change it all, quitting drinking wasn't the difficult thing to give up. Honestly, I have never given it a second thought from the moment that I decided I had to stop. But the thoughts of what I would do next, the visions of my campaigns for higher office, they haven't stopped. I was driving down the road the other day, and I had to catch myself as the visions of the next big, unhealthy dynamic of accomplishment filled my brain and gave me a taste of success, that drug I seek.

Not running for re-election was equivalent to giving up heroin because success was my drug of choice and failure was the come-down. I wished for the next high to get; instead, I went cold turkey. I could have used some version of an AA meeting there for sure: Achievaholics Anonymous. In my mind, I was crafting every way I could still run for reelection and heal myself. The truth is I couldn't do it all. I had broken the glass ceiling, and all it did was leave me bloody. That is what I didn't want to admit. That is what would label me a failure, what would make people look at me differently. And if I quit success, what would my life look like, what would define me? What would people pat me on the back for and where would the accolades come from? No awards or titles. Just me. That was a scary place to be.

## CHANGING THE SUCCESS NARRATIVE

So, after you send out a press release breaking up with your current life in a very public way, what do you do? Well, in campaigns, we would call that an opportunity to take back the message. This time, though, it was the internal message that needed to be redefined. I had to stop the chatter, the miltote as the Toltecs from my Teo spiritual work would call it, that ran in my head like a bad song you can't get out. Ever.

Alcoholics Anonymous really isn't my thing, but Achievaholics Anonymous would be my jam for sure. Regardless, though, I like many of the ideas and concepts of AA and the one they focus on a lot is one day at a time. When you are completely driven by success, all you do is look to the future and strategize how to get to that next benchmark, the next step to get you to the next step. But when you stop and focus on today, you enter a whole new space.

If I were to create this Achievaholics Anonymous, people would get a chip for every month, and then every year, that they didn't take responsibility or take on an activity based in achieving to impress others. They would be celebrated for being months clean from adding more to their plate, months in which they did not add more to their résumé and nothing to their soul.

The truth is, I should have stopped many years before, I should have got myself together, mentally and emotionally, even before I ran for City Council, but there was no time for that. The clock was ticking. You are only as young as you are at that moment, and if I was going to get elected as young as I possibly could, I had to do it that moment. My glass ceiling was the one I could see; it was right there for the taking, and I had to take it. My fear of failure was so great, so fierce, so all-consuming, that the only thing that could have jolted me out of that space was the awareness of my impending death. I had to get to that point before I realized I had a problem. That is Step 1 in my version of AA: Admitting you are powerless over the desire for success.

Now that I had identified the problem, addressing it in a meaningful way became critical. It seemed like purging at this point would be a good start. And I did. I quit a lot of my obligations because I needed a clean slate. I quit the job that I didn't really like. I wasn't really good at it, and it served as a placeholder for income, so I could afford to serve on the City Council. I had to trust this new process. I had to believe that once I eliminated the toxic need for success, the universe would fill the space with good, rich, meaningful things that brought me happiness and joy. And this turned out to be true.

I quit committees and boards. I quit networking get-togethers and endless other events that allowed me the opportunity to be seen. (I'm not going to lie, Covid was really helpful with this as well.) I started changing my boundaries with those who knew me professionally. Stress and alcohol had left my life and I lost 40 pounds quickly. I was transforming. The more I settled into this new place and pace, the more content I became. Contentment: that is the state of being I sought. I wasn't looking for the next accomplishment; I was happy right where I was, with who I was. The sadness that had been eating at my bones slowly dissolved.

I was becoming myself and watching myself emerge. What I discovered then continues to apply today. I am frank and use curse words with ease. My work uniform is my "Good moms say bad words" shirt, shorts, and flipflops, and I call it as I see it. I am authentic and more comfortable in my skin than I had ever been. I am goofy and dance poorly but often. I skip, I play, I sing (also poorly). I often have paint on my clothes because I live with my eight-year-old daughter, and I am not going to apologize. My kids' hair is never brushed, they likely don't have socks on, but they are happy. If given a chance, I will talk about travel non-stop. I laugh, belly laughs. I smile. These traits are real. I am real.

When you sit down to re-evaluate what success looks like, when you reframe your message from your heart, it's a pretty spectacular place to be.

The irony in the impulse to write a successful book about not being addicted to success is not lost on me. How do I not let the potential success of the book consume me so fully that it becomes that ever-present next thing to achieve? Awareness, though not everything, is a good thing, and these kinds of questions keep me awake to my unconscious impulses. The truth is, though, this book is, more than anything else, about the continued process toward happiness. Writing it in multiple drafts has helped me reflect, process, and heal. Ultimately, creating this book was the critical last step to allowing me to forgive my mom and being on the road to happiness. That is a pretty big deal.

In my own slice of the world, my colleagues know I didn't run for City Council, but much past that, details are slim. Because actions speak louder than words, people have seen a change, and they note it often. People frequently comment on how happy I look, and that is the best compliment they can give me. It means that I am accomplishing success for me.

A lot of my behaviors before I quit the City Council make me cringe. When we are living in active addiction, we do ugly things to ourselves, to the people we love. Even now, the narrative that I am a failure and a horrible person creeps back in, but the key to neutralizing it is making sure I stop, sit with that idea, wrap it in love and grace, and let it go. I think of the quote frequently and perhaps falsely attributed to C.S. Lewis, that "You can't go back and change the beginning, but you can start where you are and change the ending." All I have is the power to live every day differently and with more intention as a reflection of who I am. And this process makes me a better person as a mom and wife, as a political consultant, or as a citizen of the world.

Living in this new way is a daily process, a steady commitment to stay focused first on what matters for my well-being. I start by grounding myself, connecting deeply with my spirituality and hugging my kids and telling them I love them 100 times before 10 a.m. I pick work projects that align with who I am regardless of what the external political world says, engage with dear friends and family, strengthen my marriage partnership, have four trips I am planning in my head at all times, and repeat. This approach brings me happiness and contentment. And these aims, as I first pieced them together, made up the new messaging I needed to advocate for me first to find that fantastic joy.

I think back to that person who strove so fiercely to break that glass ceiling, to be the youngest woman elected to Loveland City Council, to be first to have a baby while serving. I certainly have scars from my experience. These days, when I talk about success, I focus on what it means for women, as individuals, once they have broken the glass ceilings because that act alone isn't enough. And this is what the public conversation must become. If we are truly going to make progress for women, we need to talk about what it means to support women. And women who have fought their way to unprecedented professional success need to be honest about what that battle meant for them. We don't talk about the desperately lonely aspects of the process. We don't talk enough about how lonely it can be for mothers, especially after you have a baby and the postpartum depression kicks in. We don't talk about how slashed up we get as women when we break through that glass. At least not enough. So, this is part of what success looks like for me these days: being honest about the toll the effort takes.

If as women we want to be fully integrated and have the equality we deserve, we have to be honest about the experiences we have. With the knowledge I have now and the space I am in, I will continue to push for more women to run, but we all have to be truthful about what that looks like and what must change. Moms are the best at a lot of things, including serving in public office, but the structure they are walking into is the most patriarchal of them all. Childcare everywhere has to be a priority, for instance. Meetings can have kids; meeting times can change. The rules that have been created for men in our government can and should be changed. And this only happens with more women at the table. And for women who have been there, even for just a moment, we must talk about what it means, be open and honest and authentic about the experience. We have to make it clear that doing it all is impossible and trying to doesn't make for strong, personal well-being. Honesty about the experience is what will create sustainable systematic change.

These days, the best accolade in the world is when my four-year-old son Nolan says, "Mommy, you are the best mommy in my whole world," or my Frankie makes a point to share homework or a personal admission that she doesn't have to offer, yet she does it because I have created a safe space. My heart fills when she looks at me and, with absolute sincerity, says, "I love you, Mommy." These are the relationships and accomplishments that matter, not a plaque on my wall or a line on my résumé, or my name in the local newspaper. The moments when my kids acknowledge my presence, when my choices matter most to them, and they notice: That is what success looks like to me today.

## CHANGING THE MOTHER-DAUGHTER NARRATIVE

One thing I came to realize was that if I was truly going to build an advocacy campaign for myself, I had to forgive my mom. I simply couldn't live a life of joy and happiness without forgiveness and forgiveness of the deepest kind. A good part of my need to be perfect and the most successful came from the expectations of my mom and my internal need to prove something to her, to feel as if she was proud of me and loved me. And though she might not physically be here any longer, her energy is, and that provides an opportunity for each of us to find our own way of approaching forgiveness.

Furthermore, being a mother, embracing my role as a mother and the spirit of my own daughter, was the portal into healing. Being a mother to a daughter allows me the opportunity for healing in ways I never could have imagined. As I build a strong relationship with Frankie based on love, forgiveness, understanding, and honesty, it allows me to heal my relationship with my own mother. It allows me to feel love in this mother-daughter dynamic I only dreamed of, and it allows for compassion and forgiveness I never knew possible.

When I was pregnant with each of my children, I felt an indescribable sense of connectedness with something greater than me. I had the power of the universe growing inside. They were shaping and channeling energy in me that created peace and calm, a feeling that I had strived for most of my life. Even after they were born and even through my deep struggles, that sensation lingered at the edge of my awareness, a taste of how things could be. Sometimes, as I lay Frankie or Nolan down to sleep, I would hug them so tightly it was if I was hoping to absorb them back into me. It was as if I was taking their energy and innocence and reconnecting to it all. Awareness of the energy is key, and an awareness of that constant energy makes life feel more manageable and more meaningful, maybe even more beautiful.

When I was 20 weeks' pregnant with Frankie, my mom passed away. I didn't realize it at the time, but being pregnant helped me experience peace, hope, and an awareness of the circle of life. I've only had the occasion to be with two people on their deathbed: my mom and my grandma Dorothy. I don't believe this was an accident. They were the two people who were so strongly connected to my story that it seemed necessary I was there when they passed on.

My mom's final moments were a wistful experience because I could feel the energy shifting. I could see this world being cross-lit by the next. Even though images of sunbeams may come to mind, my experience was something heavier. I now realize it was so heavy because I was absorbing, even more fully, the energy that my mom had carried with her. It was the energy of generations before her that she carried through life. This was the energy she was leaving behind, while new energy and space were being created inside of me. I wasn't sure at the moment what was happening. All I knew was it was big. The other thing I didn't fully grasp then is that I had a choice about what to do with that energy. I could keep carrying it around, or I could relinquish it, letting generations after me release the burden that had followed us for so long.

My mom had a salt lamp next to her bed, with a pile of small salt rocks neatly piled on top. The moment I realized this was her time to transition, I picked up one of those rocks, placing it in my hand and then in hers to absorb her energy to take with me and keep forever. For some reason at that moment, with this woman who had done nothing but make my life difficult, all I wanted to do was to hold onto her. Why I did it, I'm not certain, but I am grateful that I did. It would be the key to my living a life that was full of the good things and to let go of the heaviness that had been passed to me. Through this rock, I would be able to let the process of absolution grow a little bit by little bit over time.

That rock would have an impact on me in a way I couldn't have imagined during a spiritual journey to Teotihuacan five years after my mother's death. The day was clear, and rays of sun warmed my skin. As I walked down the main avenue of the pyramids, I grabbed a handful of gravel, intentionally assigning heavy burdens to the pebbles. During my walk, I dropped them one at a time, letting go of all that was weighing heavily on me: my mom, my chronic PTSD (although I didn't have that language at the time), my guilt, and my shame.

I arrived at a place that had once been a brimming river but was now reduced to a trickling stream. It smelled of sediment and rot. The air was hot. I could hear whistles from the vendors and the sounds of families enjoying the day. As I looked over the bridge, I felt my mother's salt stone in my pocket and took a deep breath. I was ready to drop this last vestige of her into the stream. That is where my hate wanted her to be. But at that moment, the energy in the stone held me back. I felt an unexpected connection to my mom through the salt. I clenched the rock tighter, and I pulled it to my heart, knowing that as much as I may have hated my mom, her heaviness did not belong in a smelly diminished river in Teotihuacan. I wondered if I could just absorb her into me as I tried with my children and maybe find the maternal love I so desperately sought from her. I thought perhaps this way I could fill my veins with light and let the weight of my suffering go once and for all. So, she stayed in my hand, and I safely tucked the rock back in my pocket. She traveled with me farther on that trip, setting the foundation of healing I desperately needed.

It's funny. My mom rarely talked about her life and owned little of her story. I wish I knew more of her story. I do remember seeing a picture of her as an apparently carefree twenty-something, ascending the exact pyramid I visited in Teotihuacan, the Pyramid of the Sun, a structure that looms large and conveys its power to visitors. Here I was, standing where she had been, holding the rock, the energy, deep in my grasp, and as I approached the pyramid, I meditated on love. As I deliberately climbed each step, placing weight first on my toes, then my whole foot, I could feel my muscles, weakened from the years of anxiety, stress, fear, guilt, and shame braided into the fiber of my being. I walked with intentionality, with purposeful forgiveness.

Once I reached the top, the view was spectacular. I could see the Toltec city for miles, with modern Mexico integrated into it. The blending of the ancestral past and the present is a powerful sight. It is as though the past energies are merging with the present ones. I became conscious of how we are all connecting the power within ourselves to the souls that came before us in an omnipresent experience that changes our DNA. It allows us to become even better spirits, better souls, with better energy. We do this not just for ourselves and not just for our children but for their children. We have the power to recognize what is deep inside us and choose differently.

And that is what I did: I chose differently. From my position on top of this pyramid, with the cave of the four-petaled flower positioned deep in the earth directly below me, a sign of birth or rebirth, a small pool of water on the top of the pyramid came into my view. At that moment, I knew what to do. I grasped the energetically heavy stone that I had been carrying for so long, which represented so much, and held my mother's energy. As I placed the stone in the water, the coolness and the smell of rain were powerful. Taking deep breaths, I rinsed the stone, set it down, and it sank to the bottom of the small puddle. This stone, this seed of forgiveness, was planted. The opportunity for new growth and a new life began.

On top of this man-made mountain, my mom and I would get a chance to start again. We would get a chance to cleanse the heavy energy that had burdened our family for so long. We would leave that heaviness for the earth to absorb, and we would find a way to heal together while being apart. Our energies connected so powerfully, they could never fully be separated, not even through death. With this place of healing and growth, we could evolve our individual energies. Together.

The stone was a real-life relic of forgiveness and change and, as I returned home to my daughter a real-life representation of an opportunity for us all to do things differently. I do not believe it was an accident that I was 20 weeks' pregnant when my mom passed away. We had the opportunity to be enriched by a new maternal soul that would guide us to healing and change our world. I am certain that at some point in that transition, my mom to her death and Frankie to her life, they crossed paths. I have images of them in my head hanging out on a cloud together in between worlds, souls passing each other.

Frankie truly is a sage. Her name comes from my maternal grandmother's maiden name, "Frank," and her middle name is my mother-in-law's, a pair of maternal blessings.

I always knew this little girl who had come into the world was a powerful source of healing. I also knew she could show me the path. But the burden was on me to pick the one that was lit with magical energy, not dark energy. Otherwise, we would likely continue to travel the troubled path of so many before us. She had a maternal gift that I could only hope to absorb. Together, she and I, and my mom, or Grandma Lola to her, were all going to break the cycle. We were going to show that even though life can be messy, ugly, scary, and hard, we can and will find a path paved in love and authenticity together, and that will mean a better future for us all.

Frequently, as Frankie and I exchange the pleasantries of a mom and a daughter, I look at her and see my small self, at three, four, five, or six years old. I am saying "I love you" to my small self, but maybe more importantly, I am saying, "I love you" to my big self. One of the greatest joys about being a parent is that I get to be the parent I wanted but didn't have. I get to hold myself accountable for the behaviors I sought in someone else. I get to change the narrative to be the loving, nurturing one that I have longed for my whole life. Not to say I don't yell at my kids or get grumpy or mad, but I get the opportunity to say, "I am sorry." We aren't perfect in any relationship, but we can admit our shortcomings and grow with each other. I can say the things to my children, and then say them to myself, too, words I never heard. "I love you." "I am sorry." These are powerful ways to take back the message in my own mind.

And something tells me my mom is on board with this reworking of how we communicate with each other. One day, when Frankie was about three, we were in the car, and out of nowhere she started crying. Alarmed, I looked back and asked what was wrong. She responded, "I miss Grandma Lola." The overwhelming shock that came over me cannot fully be explained, and I explored this feeling with her further. I never talked about my mom, so where that came from, I don't know. I could come to no other conclusion than Frankie was my guide, my connector, and my teacher to show me the path to what love could be when the channels are clear. I welcomed the messages. During this time, she told me many times, "Grandma Lola reads me stories," or "Mom, we haven't been to see Grandma Lola in a while; we need to go." And most powerful of all, and the words that I had been hungry to hear for so long, "Mom, Grandma Lola says she loves you."

Reworking the narrative can truly create healing, and once you do it, the definition of success becomes nothing other than your own. Opening portals of healing to past generations and sharing that healing and growth with the current and future generations, sitting with your authenticity and then sharing it with the world: Can you imagine how wonderful that would be?

One of the most critical elements of any campaign is a strong message. The messages that run through your head mean a lot. What you say to yourself is what you believe. It's what you internalize and what you then portray to others. One of my favorites for a long time was, "Leah, you are such a failure." Now when this thought pops into my head, I acknowledge it as something my brain wants to tell me, but then I wrap it in grace and love and let it go. I sit deeply in gratitude, running through all the things that I am thankful for that clearly are great in my life and dispel the notion that I am a failure. I recognize that is the PTSD and the addiction trying to suck me back in. I have nothing to prove, and through experience and awareness and acknowledgement, I have reclaimed the message in my own mind. I have stopped running the world's greatest negative campaign against myself, and say, "Enough! I am taking back the message for myself."

# priorities

When the self-advocacy campaign concept came to me, for a moment it seemed a little corny. But the more I sat with it, the more it worked. I know campaigns, I know my journey, and I have concluded that self-advocacy is actually the best campaign I could possibly run. And this is a clear path to accessing that overall feeling of fantastic joy.

When you are running a campaign, you are the campaign manager, and there is a focal point of that campaign. Though I am undoubtedly building a campaign and running that self-advocacy campaign for me, there is always something in life worth fighting for even beyond myself. In political campaigns, it is an issue or a candidate. Though the analogy gets a little wonky here, I see I am running an issue campaign and my kids are the issue I am fighting for. As I do the research and change my own personal message, the campaign I am running is about making myself better so I can share a richer and more meaningful life with my kids. My kids have been the thing worth fighting for.

And though the analogy may end there, one thing holds true: My kids are the center of my solar system. Once I stepped back and reevaluated how I wanted the rest of my life to unfold, they became the sun, and everything else worked around them. Of course, this didn't occur instantly. Motherhood evolves. It's not something that happens the moment you pop a kid out. Even though that makes you a mother in the literal sense, the real process is one of growth and awareness, and it is much more drawn out and it is hard.

I didn't want to have children. My husband married me under the presumption that I had no plans to have children. Ever. I had a career, I had a world to change, and I could not be bothered with the responsibilities that come with kids. To be honest, I didn't really like kids. They made me uncomfortable. I never knew what to talk with them about or how to act around them. Motherhood was just not a thing I needed to make my life complete. On a deeper level, I was afraid of what I would do to them. My mother and I had such a horrible relationship, why would I want to bring someone into the world and risk being on the other end of that same kind of situation? It seemed more humane to not have children.

One day, somewhere between my 29th and 30th birthday, that changed. I woke up and said to myself, "I want a baby." If I look at my state of mind at the time, I was grasping for hope. My mom was dying and could go at any time, and legacy was something I was thinking about. Mike had chosen to take a job that had him on the road half of the time. I was floundering a bit professionally, I had no real success as I saw it, and I hadn't found a real hook into the political world in northern Colorado. The longing to make that impact and accomplish all the things was very much present. Combining these factors with my shaky mental health, substance abuse, and unexplored trauma, things were really not that great for me. I was sad and seeking something, anything, that would make the pain I was feeling go away. It was clear what I was doing wasn't exactly working, so I was desperate to attempt anything.

When I awoke that day wanting a baby, I truly believed it was the universe's way of saying to me that I could and would find something more meaningful than what I had. There was nothing gradual or subtle about this desire, and I'm glad I was open to listening to it. When I called my husband and told him this, I am fairly certain he said something along the lines of, "Who are you and what have you done with my wife?" He had always wanted kids, but I guess at the beginning of our relationship he had decided that he was willing to compromise on that point. One of the things that I think makes our marriage work well is he always has accepted my bold personality and never once has asked me to be anything other than who I am.

When we decided that we were going to have a child, everything shifted profoundly. I started to be more aware of my surroundings and evaluate them as to how they might change. The idea that I was going to be responsible for another human being or that we were trying to make another human being felt crazy. I don't remember when I found out I was pregnant the first time, and maybe I've blocked it out because I lost that one. The first time, I told a few people, and the second time, I told even fewer. This idea that women are not supposed to talk about this extraordinary experience that is happening to them, that they have to remain silent until they are "in the clear," is loaded with sexism, patriarchy, and old ways of thinking.

When I had the miscarriage, I needed to grieve. It's a natural and necessary part of healing. The mother, the father, and the grandparents: Everyone should be able to grieve. My two miscarriages are as much a part of my motherhood story as my two living, breathing, beautiful children. They reminded me how fragile life is, how so much is out of my control, and that even though they were painful, they happened for a reason. Had I not had miscarriages my first two pregnancies, I would not have the two children I have now. I think maybe, the first time was an attempt to truly warm me up to the idea of motherhood. The second was a stark warning — which granted, I didn't listen to — that I needed to slow down. I didn't take care of myself after either miscarriage. I didn't tend to my emotional needs. All I did was put a happy face on and keep moving. Happiness was so far from what I was actually experiencing. Though I know my eyes always showed it, most people never knew the true sadness I was feeling. Grieving alone is horrible.

Then came the best part of motherhood: the kids! Being a mom is the single greatest thing about my life. When I was pregnant with Frankie, I was the healthiest I'd been as an adult. I would walk four miles a day around Lake Loveland, setting intentions for myself and my baby. As we walked all those miles, we would talk. I would consistently try to set aside expectations as I still do every day with my children. Starting that practice early was more helpful than I would ever know. It helped shape me as a parent. I have found myself pulling back the reins all the time and letting my children be the humans they are. They should not be a reflection of who I want them to be but rather a reflection of who they are at their core. Like everything that comes with parenting and really in life, I am constantly evolving, but that awareness and setting the intention of the type of parent I want to be started with those early walks around Lake Loveland.

From the beginning of being parents, Mike and I have operated fully under the belief that we should integrate the children into our lives, not the other way around. Frankie went out to dinner, she went to the political rally, and she went to the political fundraiser. She even went canvassing at eight days old. Nolan went to the National League of Cities meeting in Cleveland when he was two months old. Short of actually accompanying me to the dais for a Tuesday night City Council meeting, my kids have been and will continue to go everywhere with me. I once told women running for office with kids that I would take my kids everywhere people were comfortable having them and lots of places that people weren't. I didn't apologize then and I still will not apologize. We are never going to effectively integrate women into the political arena in a meaningful way if children aren't integrated also. The looks of discomfort when I brought my children along used to make me feel uncomfortable and even judged. But I know what I am fighting for, I know what message I am sending, and I am not going to back down.

I am not ever going to be intimidated by a stodgy old way of doing things in my pursuit for things to be different. So, as the Director of Local Affairs for the State of Colorado learned one day, dinosaur toys come with little boys to meetings, too. I left a position at a Fortune 500 company, in part because the "manager" there didn't believe children belonged in the workplace because I had brought my kids to a meeting when I had no other choice. Whether it's corporate America or the political world, women have been missing out for centuries because we have been put in a box when we have children. I have no space for that antiquated way of thinking. Women will ultimately be integrated, but it must come with a new view of children. Personally, as a mother, I know we all have to keep pushing these boundaries. Pushing boundaries shows our kids what the world should look like, not what it looks like now. I can dream with them of a world where kindness reigns and where people are not victims of patriarchy, racism, economic disparities, mental health challenges, religious discrimination, or war. Children offer us the chance to acknowledge where we are and the inspiration to do better. That is if we let them.

So much of my being a parent is deciding what factors I am going to let in. What lessons am I going to share, what truths am I going to tell or not? I know others will question and judge these decisions, but I have to do what I believe is right for my kids. I show them the macro-view of what is happening with the world and an age-appropriate micro-view of what is happening with me. Mental health challenges, my depression, and my coping with chronic PTSD are all part of who I am as a mother. The things I share with my children, from news events, to art, to movies, to philosophy and travel are also part of who I am as a mother. As I told a friend recently, of all the things I question myself about, I never ask myself whether I am a good mother. I know I am.

I am not sure when I actually decided I was a good mother. I imagine I firmly planted that flag sometime after rehab, but even before that and despite all the struggles, I still knew it deep down. I still feel guilty at times, and I don't always feel as if I am doing enough or doing it right. But even in my darkest days I still somehow found the strength to even do the most menial of things for my children. Plenty of stuff in my life is hard, like painstakingly hard, but being a mom is not one of those things. As I have settled into myself, being a mom is easy.

And releasing guilt allowed me to make motherhood fun. With mom-guilt out the window and firmly embracing the unavoidability that I am going to make mistakes, I do have one caveat. I really hate playing. I hate it. I can organize craft projects, make messes everywhere with volcanoes and glitter that madden my husband, plan and execute field trips, and take us on international adventures. I can lead my kids on hikes and nature excursions, hang out at the park, go swimming: anything but play. The words "Mommy, will you play Barbies with me?" bring up fear and guilt like nothing else in parenting for me. My behavior in this situation doesn't seem to be improving. I start to sound like a twenty-something version of myself trying to get out of a date: "I need to make dinner" or "I need to hop in the shower." The truth is, though, even as the anticipated "Mommy, you never play with me" follows, I still know in the big picture that I am doing a pretty good job. We can't all be fabulous at everything.

I have had conversations with Frankie about the challenges I face around playing. It's interesting because as I speak with truth and vulnerability, sharing my struggles with her, she seeks to understand where I am coming from and finds empathy and solutions. Of course, right after she says, "Yeah, Mom, because you aren't very good at being a kid," she adds, "Mom, I know you have a hard time playing Barbies. Let me tell you what the scene is to make it easier." Or she will say, "Mom, I know just free building LEGOs is hard for you; let's work together to build something and I will give you the idea."

Keeping focused on what matters is important, and I am reminded why my kids fit in the analogy as the cause or issue I am fighting for. They are more than anything I do, my investment in the future, my way to make the world just a little better. Creating smart, empathetic, adventurous children is quite possibly the most important gift I can give, so I focus on them more than any other cause in the world.

This awareness is vital because as I build the advocacy campaign for me, I know what is at the center, the core, the issue that I would fight more relentlessly for than anything. And when you know that, it makes everything easier. When you prioritize your life in a way that you are advocating for what is most important first, the state of joy becomes real.

# filling the bank

In politics in the United States, there is one element you need above anything else: money. You can have all the research in the world, the greatest message, and the most compelling issue and none of that will matter if you don't have money. If you don't have the resources to reach people with your message and if you lack the long-term momentum to keep that message in the forefront, you might get a good earned media hit but not much more. Filling your war chest is the task you have to make sure is in place, or the rest can't happen. There is a Democratic organization called EMILY's List. And no, it doesn't stand for some cool chick who ran for office, although I am sure there are a lot of Emilys who are cool and have run. It stands for

Early Money Is Like Yeast because a viable campaign can't be launched or sustained without it. In politics, money talks, and in self-advocacy, you need a reserve that will keep you going when that negative messaging inevitably reappears in your head.

So, in my self-advocacy campaign, when I looked at it all, the things that really filled my bank, beyond the people whom I surrounded myself with, came down to spirituality and travel. And the two are deeply intertwined in my life. Recognizing the importance of resourcing myself with those elements has been key. These components have been a part of my life at various points, but it wasn't until I stepped away from everything and rebuilt from a place of authenticity that they really intersected.

The great thing about reinventing yourself into a better version of yourself is you get to pull in the elements that bring you joy and push out the others. When I was young, travel was very present and spirituality was not. Later, as spiritually began to gain precedence in my experience, travel was just not a priority. Recently, the two have merged, allowing me an experience of growth and happiness I didn't know was possible. The merging of travel and spirituality has created resources for my brain and my soul to fill me up and allow me to serve the world in a more meaningful way.

I got to see how big the world was at a very young age because my family traveled a good deal. By the time I left for college, I had been to a dozen countries, and by the time I graduated college, that number nearly doubled. Traveling was where I felt alive, learned new things, and activated all my senses. It was what brought my soul to life.

This was quite opposite to my spiritual beliefs at this time. When I was 15, I proudly declared to my younger sister I did not believe in God. This was when we were on a family vacation in Sweden visiting distant relatives and getting ready to go to church. Younger than me by almost four years, she was distraught. How could I not believe in God? I held tightly, and rather publicly, to this belief through most of my 20s.

My family wasn't overly religious. My parents would drop us off at Sunday school and then move on to whatever they did when we were there, and that was the extent of my "religious" experience. We belonged to a United Methodist church. This denomination, I would learn later in life, allowed a broad swath of beliefs. I ultimately landed there because it offered that spiritual experience, even complete with African American hymns. It was also open to me, without judging that I thought though Jesus was a pretty cool dude, he was not in fact resurrected for my sins.

When my mom got sick, she desperately tried to find something, a meaning or belief, to grasp. She would read book after book and go on Buddhist retreats. She would buy artwork with encouraging sayings, meditate, and do yoga. At the end of her life, after my first trip to Teotihuacan, and she saw the impact it had on me and that I hadn't actually joined a cult, she asked me, "How did you find God, Leah? How did you find meaning?" I couldn't answer that then, and still can't really answer that now. Meaning is an element of the journey that I don't believe I will ever fully understand. But I will not stop seeking it.

I don't think a belief in God, the universe, or something greater comes because I want it cerebrally. I think I need to want it in my heart. It's a lot like quitting City Council or drinking. I could say I want to stop the activity that is hurting me, but I had to want the change as a part of my being, not just something that my brain said I should do. I always saw value in religion even in my most obstinate years. I would say things like, "I am jealous of people who believe. It seems like that would make life easier." But once the switch flipped, I felt the connection to something bigger than me. The more I connected with it, the more grounded I felt and the more I wanted that experience, that growth, and that way of living.

Seeking is the rich and powerful part of life. It's the desire to fill myself with more refined energy and to let the heavy energy go. When I am seeking deep spiritual experiences, that openness changes my structural makeup. Recent research in epigenetics has shown that significant changes in our emotional lives can actually repair trauma in our DNA, and I feel that to be true in my own body. Traveling does that, too; when you sit with experiences that take you out of yourself, you develop a new spatial awareness. It makes you realize you are just one small part of it all, but at the same time, you are very much part of it all, and the best way to honor your being is to dig deep into who you are and live with authenticity. To live big.

When I embraced that realization, the universe returned the favor and showed how it believed in me. This shift then was not just for me but for those before and after me. My grand-mother, my mother, and my daughter. Once this portal had been opened, the energy of healing flowed irreversibly and forever changed the life that I live and my experience in this body, in this lifetime.

The belief in God, something greater, that omnipresent experi-ence, did not exist for me until one day it did. At that moment, for whatever reason, in a flash I went from not believing to finding the majesty in daily interactions. Once I quit all the things that weren't serving my soul, the splendor of what I had instead was often more than I could have imagined. Some days, I feel as if I am living in a dream. Some days, even during our collective horrible year of 2020, I have felt so grateful, so calm, and so mesmerized by life that I just couldn't under-stand how people could be so negative.

So, in learning how to open space for the good things, I recog-nized I needed to fill my bank with travel. Before I admitted I needed a drastic change, my soul and my subconscious were helping me prepare. By opening me up to deep spiritual experiences, my internal wisdom offered me nuggets of hope over time even though I was not aware of it in my conscious-ness. The universe was laying out an exit plan from the pain and suffering I was living in, and I had to be brave enough to live it.

Before my mom died, life was heavy, I was emotionally heavy, and I knew I needed more. I dabbled in some spiritual read-ing and teachings, but I am really a hands-on learner. That is when my friend recommended a place outside Mexico City, so about six months before my mom died, I took my first adventurous, life-changing trip to Teotihuacan.

This adventure would tap into something inside of me that would never go dormant again. As a novice to ceremonies, I always feel a little uncomfortable, always look around to see if I am doing the right thing. The reality is the only right way to do it is my way, any way that allows me to slip into the space that allows me to transcend the passage of energy. The only right way is to open myself up to the opportunity of change, the kind of change that is deep in my cells, the kind of change my ancestors can feel. But there are times when I lose sight of that truth.

I think on this first trip to Mexico that I cried more than any point that I can recall. Ever. It was as if, once I allowed myself to open up and be vulnerable, I let the walls crumble and all that was there were tears. Twenty-nine years of tears that had not been cried. I cried deep in the ground in a cool damp cave as if I was inside the womb of mother earth, with the opportunity to come out in a different form as a different person. I cried over a well of sacred water, pouring all the pain into the earth for her to hold because it wasn't for me to hold any longer. I cried on top of pyramids, feeling the power of ancestral healing from those who came before me. I hadn't cried, not in a meaningful way, for years. And so, I cried.

When I stop for a moment and feel the earth under me and think about the millennia of people who walked there before me, I become aware of the power that is transmitting and the energy pulsing through my body. I connect with the earth as it really is at its core, and I feel incredibly significant and relatively insignificant all at the same time. During this first trip to Mexico, I tapped into the meaning of my role in all of this.

My soul was disrupted. It was as if a hand had disassembled a completed puzzle, and I was now trying to put it back together in a meaningful way, with intention and love. That is what this first trip did for me. All of my spiritual work from this point on was truly based on mother earth or the great mother and true ancestral healing. Even though days would get darker before they got brighter, there was a seed planted deep inside me.

Travel was something I longed to get back to, but there was just too much in my way, I was in my way. For some reason, about 15 months before I went to rehab, I had booked our first family vacation in years. I took a leap. Finances still weren't great, I was super sad, but I put my intention out there, with faith that there was something good on the horizon. And I don't think it was an accident that our travels would fall just six weeks after I withdrew from my re-election to the City Council. The universe offered me a plan B. It allowed me to see one of the primary ways I need to fill my bank.

That first family trip was magical. For eight days, Mike, Frankie, Nolan, and I were just us, deepening our relationship as a little unit of love and acceptance, but more importantly fun! Cruises are not my favorite way to travel, but it is a pretty good way to see Alaska. My children ate it up. The Alaskan coastline is breathtaking. The mountains jut straight up out of the ocean. The glaciers are nestled on peak after peak. By the end, Frankie's indifference to yet another waterfall or bald eagle was almost comical. When I travel with my kids, I want them to look at the things they should see with wonder. Nolan found his awestruck gaze in observing the light fixtures on the boat. This is a reminder that children's discoveries are theirs and theirs alone. We went whale watching and got the most spectacular show, and Nolan slept through the whole thing. We went mushing on carts with real sled dogs and got to hug the puppies. We walked along the rocky beaches and found giant starfish. We saw the beauty of the world and all its majesty: just us building a new kind of life focused on us. And that was and still is the exact, right, and most important thing I can offer.

This trip reminded me that I wanted to spend the rest of my life integrating travel into the process of deepening my spiritual core and my family relationships. It isn't just traveling for my own spiritual nourishment; it is traveling to build the kind of relationships and family structure I want: happy and healthy and full of vibrancy, adventure, and memories. This is what the renewed lease on life gave me, and I was not going to let it pass me by. I also know that traveling with my kids is a thing I want to do while they at least still like me. Traveling with little children is hard, but honestly not any more difficult than the day-to-day with them. Integrating them into my life and the world was exactly what I intended to do.

2020 hit and we all know what happened. Travel, in theory, became a thing we could only dream of, but I was not going to let that stop me. I would figure out a way to find those experiences that fed my soul and provided opportunities for amazing family growth and memories. So, I was forced to look closer to home. It turns out there are grand adventures everywhere. Looking at a map, I set out on planning a Covid-friendly trip.

We found ourselves at a ranch in Ute territory, deep in Southern Colorado, for a few days, isolated from nearly everyone except the lovely couple who own the place and a few ranch hands. There were ruins in the rocks and spirits in the air, a fertile setting for my soul to grow. We took a small trip to a spot with a ceremonial circle. Remnants of structures were strewn across the hillside. Pottery shards abounded, petrified wood sprinkled the earth, and real dinosaur bones were visible. What a treat for all of the senses and for all of us. We found a small cave in the ground where the native Utes had created a ceremonial space. I would never pass up an opportunity to go a little deeper into mother earth and come out renewed, and this time neither did Frankie.

We scaled down slowly and settled deep into the earth, feeling the stones and breathing deeply. It was cool and damp and small and silent except for our breath and our voices. I said to Frankie, "Can you feel the energy and the healing in these rocks? People hundreds of years ago did this same thing, and we get to do it now." I sat there for a moment deeply absorbing the place and losing myself in the energy. The silence was broken by, "Hey, mom, I saw a lizard. Let's go get it."

She was only six then and always on her own time. I have no doubt it took her far less time to absorb the energy than me. She is always a playful reminder that ceremony is fun, family time together is fun, and growing together and exploring it all is fun. The experiences I have with my children provide some of the deepest joy I know. I could not fully understand this, fully let it in, until I had dropped all the heavy things I was carrying from over a year before. We emerged from the ground to the welcoming light of the world, and I was reminded of the power in her little being. We never did catch that lizard.

When we returned to the ground from our time in the ceremonial hole, our lovely guide said, "The cave is very aware of energies, and no one has gone down there for a while. I offer it to every group, but for months now no one has been able to go all the way into the cave. You all did it with such ease, so thank you for opening the earth up again." The earth opened with ease for us? What a concept to treasure close to my heart and what an experience to share with my family. The powerful messages that come to us when we push outside our comfort zone are there all the time; we just have to listen.

On any self-advocacy journey, you must have the resources to keep you going. You have to find the things that fill you up. Each of us is nourished by different things: running marathons, knitting, painting, camping, volunteering, and playing chess. We have passions that allow our brains to stop dominating and our souls to take over. I have discovered that even planning trips is meditative for me. My mind feels healthier when I am planning to travel, and then my soul is replenished when I take the journey. And as my spiritual self gets folded in every time, I can feel myself filling my bank to help me be a better self-advocate, thus a better advocate for the world.

# allies

no one gets anywhere alone. Even if you are on some solitary quests, there are still powerful forces or elements helping you out: your upbringing, the weather, all of the knowledge and skills that you learned from experiences with others. You need support if you are going to push through and make meaningful changes.

I needed to ask for help and admit that I couldn't do it all on my own. We all need a village to help raise our kids, to help us move forward, and to maintain our mental health so we don't plunge into the abyss. But for years I thought it was better if I did it on my own. I kept people far enough away that they didn't know it all, believing if my world were filled with more acquaintances than friends, no one would challenge me on my destructive patterns. If I pushed my family away just enough, I thought, I could wallow in the pain and maintain the comfortable state of trauma I had become accustomed to. Help was for the weak.

Despite all that, and without knowing it, I had started preparing to ask for help for when the time was right. It began on my first spiritual journey, the first time I became aware of the universe intervening in my existence. And as I became sadder and strived more fiercely for the next accomplishment, the universe presented me with more tools that I could subconsciously use. I was thrown more ropes to grab onto so I could lift myself out of the darkness. And one of the most critical parts of that process was creating an authentic advocacy group to support me for who I was at my core and not anything to do with my relative level of success. Some had been a part of my life forever; I just had to let them in, in a new way, and others were new arrivals, but each of them was a critical component to my transformation.

## FRIENDSHIP

More than a year before I made the decision that I needed help for all my addictions, I joined a group of women around folding tables in a spiritual circle at the First United Methodist Church. Birds and bible verses were painted on the wall, and I felt like I was in my southern grandmother's living room. As the women started to talk, they described how they got to where they were, spiritually, and what they were seeking.

Themes I was not prepared for kept coming up: substance abuse and Alcoholics Anonymous.

I looked around thinking I might have walked into the wrong meeting, and had the woman who invited me not been there, I really might have thought I had. As each woman spoke, my mind raced: I am not like these women. I don't have a problem with alcohol or my drive for success. Addictions are not a thing that plagued my life, just other people's. Clearly, that was not true, but I sat there and justified it all in my mind. It turns out the woman who had started the group and became one of my dearest friends had had her struggles with alcohol and had met many of these women through Alcoholics Anonymous. Believing now more than ever that there are really no coincidences, I have no doubt I was firmly planted in that room for a reason. But that first day, I thought that if I looked them in the eyes, I would be exposed, and I was in no place for that.

There was something that made me keep giving it a try. It felt safe. Maybe, outside of my spiritual journeys in Mexico, it was the safest place I had ever found. What that room showed me for the first time in my entire life was that women who looked like me, meaning mothers, writers, social workers, substance abuse counselors, wives, daughters, and sisters, had taken on the challenge to overcome addictions and real darkness in life. Not only did they overcome it, but now they also excelled. They are amazing human beings with powerful feminine energy, and they were not apologizing for who they were. Instead, they owned it and were rocking it!

This was another one of those moments, another crumb on the journey telling me I was going in the right direction. It launched my journey with the best friends I have ever had. These women brought me into their embrace and told me it is okay to be me, my raw uncensored self, with all of the good and all of the bad. And in the beginning, I didn't even tell them all the bad. For the first year of the group, we worked through a book called *The Spiritual Journey of Motherhood*. It was a profound experience, and the weekly discussion slowly pried me open. It may have just been the last wedge in the Pandora's Box of recovery in my life that I needed. We deeply explored the relationship between spirituality and motherhood. Honestly, for me, I think they are one and the same. My own relationship with my mom, my relationship with my children, my relationship with my husband in our shared parenthood, and my relationship with these women cannot be separated. All of our energy and experiences are interconnected.

I might go so far as to say that the women in this circle saved my life. As I sat there absorbing their stories, I grew the courage in myself to ultimately ask for help. I am fairly certain, had they not been in my life, I would have killed myself. But luckily for me and the rest of the world, they were there. I told one of them a few months before I went to rehab how raw I felt on the inside, how bad it was, and that I had a problem. After her own struggles, she had become a substance abuse counselor and an extraordinary woman in her own right. She showed me great compassion. Never once did I feel shame or judgment thrust upon me from her.

She was also the same dear friend who once told me when we were talking about my career, "I don't really know what you do, and honestly I don't care." I don't know that I had ever felt so seen or valued. This group of friends offered me the opportunity to be more truly who I was than I had ever been. They pulled out an authenticity in me that I didn't know existed. Finding people who help you find the strength to advocate for yourself is the winning component to any self-advocacy campaign.

When I was in rehab, I called the woman who had started the group. She was so exuberant on the phone, I almost hung up on her because I did not share her excitement for my current life situation. She told me, "Just wait. You will be so grateful to be sober. You just don't know it yet." The act of confronting all my demons, she said, "will change your life and you will find joy!" She also matter of factly acknowledged later, "You went to rehab more to give up City Council than anything," recognizing how deeply impactful my addiction to success was in my story and how important it was these women support me for that.

She was right about it all.

These women came and visited me while I was going through rehab. While I was thinking my life was over if anyone found out, that thought was in the external world where I felt pressures and expectations, judgment and shame. But, in this new internal world I was building, these women made me feel safe, and their feelings were welcome, they encouraged my authenticity, and we celebrated our genuineness. In the first days, during the rawest moments, I wanted those women to empower me to be the person I knew and they knew was deep inside. Masked by years of trauma, a new woman was just bursting to come out.

I call these women my coven sisters, and together we perform spells of the heart and voodoo of the soul. They are my sanctuary where I am never afraid to be who I am. They are my travel partners and my spiritual guides. They celebrate with me. They care only about who I am. I have never had a place in life where I felt 100 percent like that. They gave me a gift of learning what true advocates for my soul looked like, what unfiltered friendship felt like, and that in itself is as deeply spiritual as I get.

## LOVE

Mike and I met at a happy hour. I had moved back to Loveland because my mom's cancer had come back. I ran into a guy from high school who invited me out after work. He said Mike would be there, asking if I remembered him. I did not. We were in the same graduating class, but the joke between Mike and me now is that I went to high school enough for the both of us. We were different, very different. But the moment I saw him, I knew there was something. I have never felt such an instantaneous connection.

So, our story began. Mike made me laugh. He allowed me to be myself in a way I hadn't experienced. He said I made bad dancing look good and told me over and over to stop caring what people thought of me. I remember just weeks into our relationship looking at engagement rings and picking wedding dates. Getting married wasn't really on my radar at that point, but it seemed the time had come. I had always had a thing for the number three. I played a Titleist 3 golf ball in every tournament I had entered since I was 12. It was my magic number. Looking at the calendar, September 3, 2011, was just a year and a half away, and that was the day we decided to marry.

We grew close quickly. He felt safe to me and, in some ways, became a refuge for the constant berating I received from my mother. Because we now lived only five miles apart, her wrath had intensified with the increased proximity. I had set out on my journey of ambition and success in Loveland, and Mike supported me every step of the way. At times, he gently questioned why, but he always let me be Leah and do my thing. Part of our agreement is we each do us, good or bad, and then there is growth and forgiveness.

He has seen me as I am since the moment we met. This also means he has seen the worst of me. He felt the sting of my struggles. There were times when I hurt him terribly. I tried to pull away from his unconditional love and go deep into the darkness. He would dig deeper than the pain and hurt to come out on the other side with unconditional love every time.

At times, I have felt I didn't deserve Mike's love, but the truth is we deserve that quality of unwavering commitment. The people who love us at this level also deserve our devotion in return. For years, I know our contributions to the relationship were not a 50/50 split, but today I sit with such deep gratitude for who Mike is, what he went through with me, and how he never wavered from his role as an advocate for me, the life we had, and the life we continue to build together.

There is a truism in politics: There are many chances to say the thing. The same is true of life, but it only works when the listener is listening. The universe gave me the most loyal and ardent love, and Mike has never wavered from that role. And although it took a lot of work to get there, when the final opportunity to say enough to my trauma-driven way of life came forward, I took it. I landed in the safe place Mike offered, a place that I will forever call home.

## FAMILY

In my family of origin, my mom dominated. Her unhappiness, her demand for perfection, and her reprimands commanded so much of my attention that my dad and my sister sometimes seem like extras in the memories. When she got sick, my mom's illness took center stage over everything. Right after I graduated from college, she began an eight-year battle with cancer. Because she served on the local school board, her illness became public, and I was full of feelings of obligation and guilt given our complex relationship. As each of us sorted through our own demons and our own relationships to my mom, I realized how important my dad and my sister were. It became clear to me that any family relationship you can salvage can be so important. Family isn't supposed to give up on you, and though they certainly didn't like where I was in life, my dad and sister never stopped loving me.

When I finally said that's it, I needed help, there was no one better positioned to support me than my father. There is a reason I said to Mike, "Call my dad. I want to go tonight."

My dad had called the rehab facility, and the personnel said, I would have to come in the morning. Not accepting that answer and intuiting that I might not be resolute in my decision in the morning, he picked me up and off we went.

When we got there, he worked his magic, not accepting "Wait until morning" as an answer. I sat in the car waiting, and soon enough, a nurse was helping me into the facility. Unlike my mom, Dad was not defensive about the plight of my life. He knew the immense pressure I put on myself, my mother and my poor relationship, or that I was raped. He knew these things and, for years, didn't know how to help. Now, he could help; now I was giving him permission to advocate for me, a role he had longed for. The best kind of advocates need to be invited in and empowered to fight for your well-being. Pushing away key supporters will never allow you to build an advocacy network for your personal success, but being aware enough to know this is not an easy feat.

That was a pivotal moment. I had to ask my dad and my sister through my words and my actions to be a part of my life again, be in my corner, and be my advocate

As for my sister, when I quit the addictions and moved on in this new state of being, it took time. We had a very different relationship with my mom, and as I explored and healed, being aware of her dynamic with my mom was vital. But one thing I knew was that, despite it all, she would be there if I asked.

Sometimes, activating your advocacy network comes through admitting you are sorry. And you don't even have to say the words exactly. Amends can be in your actions. That is how it went with my sister, and now she sits firmly ready to be a part of the advocacy network I need. I cherish that little family unit of my sister, my dad, and me navigating this life without my mom, with a lot less drama. Family can be the toughest of the allies and the biggest adversaries, sometimes at the same time. But without them, the strength of history and legacy and empowerment from those you've known the longest is lost.

You need people in your corner no matter what you do as you build a campaign for self-advocacy. I know my supporters, and as I set priorities in my life, right after my children come these extraordinary people. We need to know people are cheering us on, and now more than ever, I know people are celebrating me for the person I am authentically. That feels pretty fantastic.

Self-advocacy campaigns are built on a foundation of the people who you will allow to be there for you. They are built on people who love you and see you for who you are. They support you through the challenges and love you through the tribulations. They are there when you fall to help you dust off and evaluate where to go next. The best campaigns are built on grassroots networks and influential people willing to lift you up and fight alongside you for a shared mission. My allies, my people, have helped me pick myself back up and put it all together again, to be my best and most powerful self. Finding your people is a powerful tool for self-advocacy.

# campaign manager of success

n a community meeting the other day, I shared my points and discovered I was choking back tears. The matter we were discussing was of grave importance in my community, and I saw change happening quickly that I felt was bad. A process was moving toward more bureaucracy and decreased grassroots engagement, and these shifts were emerging from a need to consolidate and make things easier for an organization, but it was not better for the people it served. Though emotion over the years has no doubt been heard in my voice, it hasn't been that visible.

Afterward, I felt a tinge of embarrassment. Where did those tears come from? Why couldn't I keep myself together and present the strength I wanted to convey? The truth was, strength wasn't the issue. Vulnerability was. This was an issue that impacted my community greatly, and strength wasn't the tool to guide the conversation. The emotion, I realized, came from two places: a grounded sense of my values and an authenticity the world was just going to have to get used to.

The matter brought up deep emotion because it was truly important. To gloss over it with feigned strength would have obscured the critical significance of the issue we were debating. And now as I sit in a place of grounded confidence, it strikes me that this is who I have been as a woman trying to make a difference in the world and doing so in a way that doesn't send me to an early grave. At this point, the only thing I know how to do is be authentically myself, and when it comes to my professional life in politics, that is what I am going to do. I honestly think we would all be better off looking inward as we make decisions rather than react to external factors.

I have to remember that whatever I work on externally, whatever projects I take on, I get the final say in my involvement. I am in charge of how my work integrates into my life. We can create a fluid model that allows us to be good humans working for what we believe in. But this realization hasn't come easy to me.

Professionally I have been defined as a Democrat for all of my career, but sometimes I just have no idea what I am, and all the while know what I am not: a Republican. My own personal identity crisis in politics certainly made grounding myself more challenging. I have been a Democrat since before I could vote. I always joked I was the kid on *The Breakfast Club* that got a fake ID so he could vote. That journey started in my freshman year civics class when we took a quiz to see where we landed on the political spectrum.

> Do you believe a woman should have access
> to abortion care no matter the situation?
> **Yes.**

> Do you believe that minorities
> should be given additional
> opportunities to ensure equality?
> **Yes.**

> Do you believe public dollars should pay
> for art that some may think is offensive?
> **Yes.**

> Do you believe in government
> social programs to help those
> that are less fortunate?
> **Yes.**

> Do you believe that tax structures should
> aid and help the poor and middle class?
> **Yes.**

I landed firmly as a Democrat. Identifying this way put me in a box that created a channel for success, but it also left little room to define myself in other ways. Over time, people change, our parties change, and I have come to wonder in the last decade if I really am a Democrat. I find I firmly believe about 60 percent of the platform of the party, but often, I don't feel my moderate beliefs are welcome in the party. It seems I'm not woke enough, I'm not progressive enough, I don't fight for the right issues in the right ways. I'm not going to lie and for a political operation that purports to strive for inclusivity, the Democratic party sure seems to operate to the detriment of the many they aren't including. Part of the reason I remain a Democrat is that I am personally so socially liberal. I believe love is love, I believe vehemently in a woman's right to choose, and I believe we have to help people and help them rise. I proudly attended BLM rallies, and I believe in a diverse representation. Yet I am fiscally conservative. This seeming contradiction means there is not much of a home for me in politics.

Since I decided not to run for re-election, I think I have become even stronger in my sense of self and my political beliefs. I am over being put in a box limiting what I should believe in my politics. I am going to support what is best for my community, political party aside. That is why come election time, there will be Democrats and Republican yard signs in my front yard because the boxes clearly aren't doing us any good.

As I sat down to write this book, knowing I was in a deep, crazy political identity crisis, I had to know where I belonged. The only place I could think of that could provide this clarity was the Internet. I took political spectrum tests, and they all came back the same. I was a moderate Democrat. It was a kind of relief to have the Internet confirm my doubts and fears, but it certainly didn't help on a pragmatic level because the world we live in does not welcome moderation.

When I worked in Washington, D.C., over 15 years ago, my far more progressive colleagues would often look at me in the scope of a conversation and say, "Ah, you are such a western Democrat." At the time, western Democrats only voted with the party 60 percent of the time. I still get comments in my work on a weekly basis that come from both sides. "Oh, you are such a liberal." "With your stance on business, how do you call yourself a Democrat?" People have done a great job over the years making assumptions about my beliefs, and I think my colleagues in Washington, D.C., might have been the ones to get it right. Just a moderate Democrat over here, with a desire to find solutions that change the world.

With this Internet confirmation, my political identity crisis was solved. With my hard-won grounded strength and authenticity, I knew there was an opportunity. When you work in U.S. politics, only two teams exist. And participants are pushed to pick a team. But I am not willing to accept that; I am not willing to believe that politics has to be so much of a zero-sum game that you can't have friends or get things accomplished with people from the other side. It is false, and as a country, we need to stop tolerating that premise. We are more than that, we are better than that, and I will continue to fight for nothing more than balance and moderation in our system.

A learned experience through being on City Council reaffirmed this belief more than anything. When I ran for City Council in Loveland, the old white men who had occupied those seats forever worked very hard to make sure the

"Boulder Liberal Leah," who was coming to push a progressive agenda, did not get elected. Once elected, I had two choices: Hold grudges against these conservatives who worked hard not to get me elected, or don't and see what I could get done. I quickly dropped the resentments I could have held, rolled up my sleeves, and went to work. And I did the unthinkable: I made friends with these old white men.

And you know what happened? We got things done. The most notable was passing an affordable housing agenda they likely never would have supported had I not built the relationships necessary for them to understand my point of view. The conversations I had with these men were meaningful, and I would say that when things got the worst for me, with postpartum depression and ramifications from years of unchecked PTSD, they stepped up and supported me in ways I never expected. These supposed political enemies helped me find experts. They made it so I could still do my job despite the intense pain and suffering I was facing. They were compassionate, and they were friends. A far cry from the narrative we are told in the media. A far cry from the narratives both major party structures tell us to keep power dynamics in place. The reality was simply a group of humans, politics aside, helping each other succeed.

What made it more perplexing was that the party that was supposed to be supporting me as a young mother in politics abandoned me, even planning to run someone against me. The local "Democrats" never bothered to check in on my state of being, after I had just broken a glass ceiling. For them, it was about the next win. The people who were supposedly against the concept of young mothers being elected altogether were the ones lifting me up. Let that sink in because, honestly, I still can't wrap my head around it. It didn't fit the narrative I was told and proved once again for me that nothing is black and white in politics, and things are often not what they seem. What I learned from that moment forward was I couldn't keep doing things the same way. And I was going to do my best to build my own narratives because the external ones in politics right now are the narratives of a power structure and not the narratives of reality.

What I grasped through that experience and now what I apply in my life is that people learn nothing when we talk at them. It's like talking at people's addiction: They are never going to listen. Who wants to hear they are wrong or are bad, intolerant people?

With this grounding belief, authenticity, and new revelations, the question becomes: What do I do? I know I stand on the shoulders of generations of women in this country who have fought to have a place in the political arena. These courageous forebearers created the opportunity for me to sit at the table in the first place, but I think I would be doing them a disservice if I didn't talk about my lived experience once I was at the table. Telling the truth about our lives is a way to ensure all women are supported, and it helps us alter the experience of public service so the structures don't break them while they are there. Sitting at the table simply isn't enough anymore. The whole well-being of women when they are there is the next step, and that change only happens if we talk about it.

With the insight derived from the campaign that I had built for myself, now I had an opportunity: Make my career in politics what I wanted on my terms. Sounds awesome, right? Or unreasonable? Or downright insane in our current system? I'll go with insane, but the last time I checked the definition of insanity, it was doing the same thing over and over again without a change in the results, and I have no plans for the latter part of my political career to look like the former. I want to work for solutions. I want to work for sanity, pragmatism, and leadership that brings about convening and compromise.

Even though I will fight like hell for what I believe in, people with passionate beliefs on the other side can make valid points, too. They come to their beliefs through their own life experience as I have. And though I may think I am right, I do want to compromise and I seek to understand the opposite view. It helps if I see those people as humans. Then we find solutions.

When I left national politics, I was disillusioned by the fact that so much of what I did was rooted in the fallacy that we were right and they were wrong. When I came home and started organizing around concerns that mattered to the community, it was clear that issues I fought for weren't partisan. Revitalizing downtowns isn't a Democrat or Republican issue, job creation on a community level is not a partisan issue, and whether your trash gets picked up, your lights turn on, or your potholes are filled shouldn't be a partisan issue. I don't think we are going to fix the division at the top if we don't start at the grassroots level. For so long I believed I needed to change the World, Capital "W." The truth is all I can do is change my world. Lowercase "w."

And so, as I redefine my role in politics, I am on a quest to create and participate in systems that support moderate candidates. I believe, with all my heart (and polling tells us), that is where the country is. So, at this point, I work for moderate Democrats and moderate Republicans to get elected because they are willing to have the conversations we need if we want to see things get done. Otherwise, our country will not survive.

Being the campaign manager of my own life means I determine what I work on and how I approach it. And I bring nothing but authenticity to what I do, with a grounded and unwavering confidence. This steadiness keeps me rooted and extends into what I make happen outside myself.

A campaign manager decides it all. She is the air traffic controller of all the moving parts. And this is the thing: As I took back control of my life, I saw how the professional arena was pretty darn important. It was the channel that created the opportunity for endless success. Through my political pursuits, I could keep pushing and pushing until my own demise. Now, in my professional life, I still strive to change my world, but I maintain healthy boundaries around who I am, and work for a system, with my unicorn beliefs, that I believe is possible.

# winning

Winning. Such a loaded word. When someone wins, it means that someone else loses. That has been the business I have been in my whole career. But though we need the people to do the work of elected officials, our focus should not be on winners and losers. It should be on policy, the laws and governance that come through moderation.

Looking at my own journey, the need to win has driven everything because winning has meant success.

For so long, my fear of failure kept me in that vicious cycle of striving for success and filling the gaps in the middle with secondary addictions until my death would become the other option. As I write, I still can't fully comprehend the enormity of it; my drive for success and to be perfect (which clearly, I was so far from) was so great that I drove myself to the brink.

So, what do I do if success is based simply on who I am and not the deeds that I have done?

In my new version of myself, I am in a stronger place than I was ever before to advocate for the things that matter to me because I know what I believe. My actions come from a place of happiness, contentment, and the right motivations. When people tell me profound societal transformation is not possible, I say, if I could travel to the depths of the abyss and come back to tell my tale, if I can take that strength and push for change in my community, country, and world, isn't anything possible? And don't we all deserve that chance to reinvent ourselves in a more meaningful, authentic, and loving way?

For four solid years, of which I was in the worst state of my existence, I had City Council meetings every Tuesday night. Every Tuesday night, week in and week out, I would kiss my family goodbye at 5:30 p.m. and know it would be hours before I returned home. I would miss my children's bedtime and often miss it many more times in a week due to other meetings. City Council controlled my life and made me miss moments. That sinking feeling in my stomach was there often and started right from the beginning. The night I was sworn in, Frankie had a stomach bug. I had planned to have her go and see this glass ceiling breaking moment, but the reality became something quite different. As I left her with my mother-in-law, I was choking back tears and fighting that pit in my stomach that I was picking the wrong thing. But I went, and I did the thing that gave me the accolades I felt I so desperately needed.

It turns out that after I quit the City Council, Tuesday nights became something of a sacred time, a time of the week when I was more intentional than ever about the activities I was doing. Summer months came, and on Tuesday nights, we would sit at the pool. I watched as my kids embodied the sheer joy of childhood, playing, laughing, and splashing in the water. The basicness of sitting in a hard, upright, outdoor chair soaking in the vitamin D as the sun set in the background over the mountains and the sunbeams shimmered over the water was magical. Occasionally, I would let my mind wander to how my Tuesday nights used to be: Trying to prove something I never had to prove in the first place. Then I would look around and soak in the moment and be grateful we all get the opportunity to reinvent ourselves.

My intentionality around Tuesday nights hasn't changed: no meetings after 5 p.m. and quality time with my little family unit that gives me so much joy. Shortly after I left the City Council, I bought a sign for our kitchen that says, "We dance in this kitchen." And boy do we ever: Tuesday, Wednesday, Thursday nights, dance parties abound, and there is nothing better in my mind then dancing with a clear head and small children. It brings an unadulterated sense of joy that truly is unmatched. I often think as my rhythmless being flails around our kitchen and living room, screaming, "This is what life is about. This is what matters."

And it's with that same intentionality I face nearly everything in my life these days. What matters most comes first; then the rest, well, it's just the rest. It certainly doesn't mean I am personally winning a campaign with my name on the ballot or an award you may read about in the paper, but the truth is the rewards I have discovered on this side of the journey aren't going to be in the paper. The awards I am getting now are the ones of a person who found a tempo and a rhythm that makes life enjoyable and leaves plenty of time for dance parties in the kitchen.

And with my belief that my priorities were sorted out, one thing that is clear is a lot of what brings me joy is motion: dancing, traveling, the next craft project, the next birthday party. But in all this action of finding fantastic joy, something I am attempting to do better is sitting, soaking in the moment. Sometimes, I have been lucky enough to sit for a few moments and reflect on the sea of gratitude I float on every day and relish how good life really is. And then there are the moments where I can sit even a little longer and slip into a reflective state that makes me almost float.

About a year and a half after the press release went out, I went on the first family vacation with my whole family: dad, sister, and crew. We rented an Airbnb on the Mayan Riviera Coast. It was a place near the rest of the world, that forced you to slow down. There was nothing to do but eat, sleep, swim, walk on the beach, and sit. And sit is what I did. In perhaps one of the most uneventful, but majestically perfect weeks, I got a moment to sit in a beach chair, feel the cool ocean breeze, and hear the chorus of crashing waves and palm trees rustling.

As I sat there, I fell into a transcendental space. In a dream-like state. I found myself in an older house. I moved through each empty and freshly painted room. Each room had large windows facing an almost New England summer beach scene. I moved from one naturally lit room to the next as if I was taking a tour to move into the place.

Later, as I was reflecting on the "dream" I had, it occurred to me how much it was a sign from the universe I was right where I needed to be. I had cleared out all these rooms in my life, and now they were freshly painted, ready for the new elements of my life to fit into the old structure. A little remodel, I suppose you might say. Or really more like a blank slate, a new place to start, to reinvent who I am from the inside out.

Reflecting on how far I have come gives a whole new meaning to winning. And with the ability to admit the distance I was from perfection, I can strive to live out the campaign to advocate for my own joy. I have assembled the key things in life, like finding my passions and filling my bank, and I base my priorities on what is important, consistently creating an internal narrative that is positive and joyful. I know who my advocates are, and I have dug deep into the ghosts of trauma past (my own and those from generations before me). Intentionally embracing all of these elements changes things, and it has wholeheartedly changed me.

What should people think of the raw, unfiltered, faulted Leah? A person who spent the majority of her life living in the depths of sadness only to come out on the other end, happier, more content? As I look at all of my flaws, I celebrate them. I often wonder if people tire of my authenticity, but the truth is, I don't really care. I can now own the fact that I just don't have my shit together, and I am simply doing the best I can. I am okay with who I am and what I am capable of, and I am not trying to be anything that I am not. I don't care what people think of me, and I am content with where life has brought me and the story I have to tell. The real joy is in knowing this isn't the end of my voyage but rather a new beginning.

Winning in this case is my writing this book. Winning is quitting the City Council and reevaluating what success meant for me. Winning is that I have forgiven my mom. Winning is my kids getting a healthier, happier mother in me, who broke generations of the trauma cycle. Winning is the unexpected and astonishing fact that I am still here. Winning is all of us being honest and authentic and sharing about what our own life experiences mean. It is overcoming challenges together in our political system and our own lives.

Winning is knowing there are hard days, and at times, I will feel sad, I will lose my patience with my children, and everything will not always go my way. But my existence is no longer rooted in the deepest, darkest sadness. Rather, I live most of my time in an elevated state, a place of fantastic joy, and that is a win that makes navigating the journey of life a whole lot easier.

# acknowledgments

There are so many people to thank who are part of this story in one way or another. Some I haven't directly mentioned in these pages, but they have made the journey, even for a moment, a little bit better, a little bit easier.

My family: Mike, Frankie, and Nolan. My extended family: my dad, my sister and her husband Jordan, and his mom, Patty. Thank you and I love you.

My coven: Megan, Jessica, Jill, Robyn, Allison, Kristen, Sarah. Thank you for showing me the meaning of friendship.

My spiritual Sherpas: Emily G, Iva, and Heather. Thank you for connecting me to the power of the universe.

My dear friends over the years: Pam, Dana, Amy, Judy, Will, Ryan, Jonah, and Ira. Thank you in your moments for being the people I needed.

My mentors and colleagues: Tom, Scott M., Scott R., John, Rob S., Cara, Muthoni, Sarah. Thank you for being great mentors and friends.

And not to be forgotten are the people who helped make the idea of this book a reality: Cyndi as well as the team at Modern Wisdom Press. Thank you for helping me give my story a voice.

# thank you

———

Thank you, dear reader. Thank you for engaging in my story, in my journey. Thank you for being vulnerable with me.

Life can be hard, and really terrible things happen, but that doesn't mean we have to become those things. Together with storytelling and the power of authenticity, we can all find paths that lead us to fantastic joy. It's possible to find the place where the bad things don't control your general state of being. You can learn to live with your trauma in an elevated state that still allows you to experience happiness and joy.

I invite you to visit my website www.findingfantasticjoy.com and download the "Self-advocacy Campaign Plan." This is a real-life guide for you to use elements of this book and reflect on changes and priorities in your own life, a plan for you to build a self-advocacy campaign of your own and find your own unfiltered joy.

Here's to the journey of finding fantastic joy. I find it daily now, and my deepest wish is that you do, too!

Much Gratitude,
Leah

# about the author

―――

Leah Johnson's résumé includes the words Obama, Kay Hagen, and City Councilwoman, but what she has come to find out is that "mom" is the best title she's ever added to her résumé. After a career that fueled her addiction to success and other things, life was dark, and something had to change. Forced to take a step back, she re-evaluated her priorities and started fresh in many ways.

Now she lives with a freedom to be herself and know how far from perfect she is. As an imperfect mother of two, she sometimes says bad words, frequently forgets to pack snacks for preschool, and on occasion, her kids eat popsicles for breakfast. But she knows she is doing the best she can, and that is all people can do on their journey. She had a whole lot of traumas early in life that made the middle part tough. But through an intense spiritual awakening, a reevaluation of priorities, and kicking a few addictions, Leah has confronted her trauma, has found a way to pull herself out of the depths of sadness, and is now on a powerful journey of self-advocacy in pursuit of finding fantastic joy.

Leah grew up in Loveland, Colorado, and has an undergraduate degree from Boston University, and half of a master's degree in Public Policy and Administration from Northwestern University (because, well, sometimes you just don't finish things). She has had a 20-year career in campaign politics and public affairs. Her little family unit is everything to her, and she spends every free moment she can with them traveling the world or having dance parties in their kitchen.